THE
QUOTABLE MANAGER
INSPIRATION FOR BUSINESS AND LIFE

COMPILED BY JOEL WEISS

Gibbs Smith, Publisher
Salt Lake City

First Edition
10 09 08 07 06   10 9 8 7 6 5 4 3 2

Text © 2006 Joel Weiss

Published by
Gibbs Smith, Publisher
P.O. Box 667
Layton, Utah 84041

Orders: 1.800.748.5439
www.gibbs-smith.com

Designed by Martin Yeeles
Printed and bound in Korea

Library of Congress Cataloging-in-Publication Data
The quotable manager : inspiration for business and life / [edited by] Joel
Weiss.— 1st ed.
      p. cm.
  Each chapter begins with a brief biography of the well-known person who
exemplifies the subject.
  Includes index.
  ISBN 1-58685-768-1
  1. Executives—Conduct of life. 2. Businesspeople—Conduct of life.
3. Leadership—Quotations, maxims, etc. 4. Management—Quotations,
maxims, etc. 5. Business—Quotations, maxims, etc. I. Weiss, Joel (Joel J.)

HD38.2.Q67 2006
658.4'09—dc22

2005025805

CONTENTS

IF

IF YOU CAN KEEP YOUR HEAD WHEN ALL ABOUT YOU

ARE LOSING THEIRS AND BLAMING IT ON YOU;

IF YOU CAN TRUST YOURSELF WHEN ALL MEN DOUBT YOU,

BUT MAKE ALLOWANCE FOR THEIR DOUBTING TOO;

IF YOU CAN WAIT AND NOT BE TIRED OF WAITING,

OR, BEING LIED ABOUT, DON'T DEAL IN LIES,

OR BEING HATED DON'T GIVE WAY TO HATING,

AND YET DON'T LOOK TOO GOOD, NOR TALK TOO WISE;

IF YOU CAN DREAM—AND NOT MAKE DREAMS YOUR MASTER;

IF YOU CAN THINK—AND NOT MAKE THOUGHTS YOUR AIM,

IF YOU CAN MEET WITH TRIUMPH AND DISASTER

AND TREAT THOSE TWO IMPOSTORS JUST THE SAME;

IF YOU CAN BEAR TO HEAR THE TRUTH YOU'VE SPOKEN

TWISTED BY KNAVES TO MAKE A TRAP FOR FOOLS,

OR WATCH THE THINGS YOU GAVE YOUR LIFE TO, BROKEN,

AND STOOP AND BUILD 'EM UP WITH WORN-OUT TOOLS;

IF YOU CAN MAKE ONE HEAP OF ALL OF YOUR WINNINGS

AND RISK IT ON ONE TURN OF PITCH AND TOSS

AND LOSE, AND START AGAIN AT YOUR BEGINNINGS,

AND NEVER BREATHE A WORD ABOUT YOUR LOSS;

IF YOU CAN FORCE YOUR HEART AND NERVE AND SINEW

TO SERVE YOUR TURN LONG AFTER THEY ARE GONE,

AND SO HOLD ON WHEN THERE IS NOTHING TO YOU

EXCEPT THE WILL WHICH SAYS TO THEM: "HOLD ON!"

IF YOU CAN TALK WITH CROWDS AND KEEP YOUR VIRTUE

OR WALK WITH KINGS—NOR LOSE THE COMMON TOUCH,

IF NEITHER FOES NOR LOVING FRIENDS CAN HURT YOU,

IF ALL MEN COUNT WITH YOU, BUT NONE TOO MUCH;

IF YOU CAN FILL THE UNFORGIVING MINUTE

WITH SIXTY SECONDS' WORTH OF DISTANCE RUN,

YOURS IS THE EARTH AND EVERYTHING THAT'S IN IT,

AND—WHAT IS MORE—YOU'LL BE A MAN, MY SON!

Rudyard Kipling
1865 1936
A famous English author & Nobel Prize winner in 1907

INTRODUCTION

The quote captures an idea or teaching in a few words—concisely and with impact.

For example, Benjamin Franklin's famous expression, "Early to bed and early to rise, makes a man healthy, wealthy, and wise." Simple, meaningful, useful and easy to remember.

The quotes are divided into twenty topical chapters. A brief biography of a well-known person who exemplifies the topic introduces each chapter.

The quotes were gathered from the Internet and public writings, available for everyone.

J. Weiss

ATTITUDE

MARGARET THATCHER, the first woman to be elected prime minister of England, became one of the most important leaders of the world in the twentieth century.

Thatcher entered Parliament when she was thirty-four and worked her way up to be the education minister. In 1975 she chanced a run for her party's leadership against Edward Heath and won in an upset.

When Thatcher took office as prime minister in 1979 she was faced with a dismal economy and bitter labor relations. She knew that socialism had to be reversed and that meant some dramatic changes. Thatcher wanted less government intervention, fewer taxes, fewer public expenditures, more power to the individual and more private ownership. She had to fight inflation, high interest rates and a recession.

Through difficult times and the risk of political failure, it was Thatcher's positive attitude and willpower that helped her achieve her goals and become a leader in the move to privatize nationalized industries.

Additionally, Thatcher partnered with President Reagan to put pressure on the U.S.S.R. to reform under Mikhail Gorbachev. This pressure contributed greatly to the eventual fall of the Berlin wall and the dissolution of the U.S.S.R.

Margaret Thatcher served as the prime minister from 1979 until 1990, longer than any continually serving prime minister in 150 years.

YOU MAY HAVE TO FIGHT A BATTLE MORE THAN ONCE TO WIN IT.

Margaret Thatcher

NOTHING CAN STOP THE MAN WITH THE RIGHT MENTAL
ATTITUDE FROM ACHIEVING HIS GOAL; NOTHING ON
EARTH CAN HELP THE MAN WITH
THE WRONG MENTAL ATTITUDE.

Thomas Jefferson

1743–1846, Third President of the U.S.

NO PESSIMIST EVER DISCOVERED THE SECRET OF
THE STARS, OR SAILED TO AN UNCHARTED LAND,
OR OPENED A NEW DOORWAY FOR
THE HUMAN SPIRIT.

Helen Keller

1880–1968, American Author, Educator

NOTHING GREAT WAS EVER ACHIEVED WITHOUT ENTHUSIASM.

Ralph Waldo Emerson

1803–1882, American Poet, Essayist

ALTER YOUR ATTITUDE AND YOU CAN ALTER YOUR LIFE.

Unknown

MOST PEOPLE SEARCH HIGH AND WIDE FOR THE KEYS TO
SUCCESS. IF THEY ONLY KNEW THE KEY TO THEIR DREAMS
LIES WITHIN.

George Washington Carver

1864–1943, American Horticulturist, Chemist, Educator

CERTAIN THOUGHTS ARE PRAYERS. THERE ARE MOMENTS
WHEN, WHATEVER BE THE ATTITUDE OF THE BODY,
THE SOUL IS ON ITS KNEES.

Victor Hugo

1802–1885, French Poet, Novelist, Dramatist

SO OF CHEERFULNESS, OR GOOD TEMPER . . . THE MORE
IT IS SPENT, THE MORE IT REMAINS.

Ralph Waldo Emerson

1803–1882, American Poet, Essayist

THINGS TURN OUT BEST FOR THE PEOPLE WHO MAKE THE BEST
OUT OF THE WAY THINGS TURN OUT.

Art Linkletter

b. 1912, American Radio Broadcaster, Television Personality, Author

IT IS OUR ATTITUDE AT THE BEGINNING OF A DIFFICULT TASK WHICH, MORE THAN ANYTHING ELSE, WILL AFFECT ITS SUCCESSFUL OUTCOME.

William James

1842–1910, American Philosopher, Psychologist

EACH OF US MAKES HIS OWN WEATHER, DETERMINES THE COLOR OF THE SKIES IN THE EMOTIONAL UNIVERSE WHICH HE INHABITS.

Fulton J. Sheen

1895–1979, American Catholic Bishop

THE PRINCIPLE OF ALL SUCCESSFUL EFFORT IS TO TRY TO DO NOT WHAT IS ABSOLUTELY THE BEST, BUT WHAT IS EASILY WITHIN OUR POWER, AND SUITED FOR OUR TEMPERAMENT AND CONDITION.

John Ruskin

1819–1900, English Writer, Art Critic, Architecture Critic

YES, YOU CAN BE A DREAMER AND A DOER TOO, IF YOU WILL REMOVE ONE WORD FROM YOUR VOCABULARY: IMPOSSIBLE.

Robert H. Schuller

b. 1926, American Reformed Church Minister, Entrepreneur, Author

HE WHO KNOWS OTHERS IS LEARNED. HE WHO KNOWS HIMSELF IS WISE.

Lao Tzu

b. 600 BC, Chinese Taoist Philosopher

EVERY JOB IS A SELF-PORTRAIT OF THE PERSON WHO DID IT. AUTOGRAPH YOUR WORK WITH EXCELLENCE.

Unknown

IF YOU WOULD ATTAIN TO WHAT YOU ARE NOT YET, YOU MUST ALWAYS BE DISPLEASED BY WHAT YOU ARE. FOR WHERE YOU ARE PLEASED WITH YOURSELF THERE YOU HAVE REMAINED. BUT ONCE YOU HAVE SAID, "IT IS ENOUGH," YOU ARE LOST. KEEP ADDING, KEEP WALKING, KEEP ADVANCING; DO NOT STOP, DO NOT TURN BACK, DO NOT TURN FROM THE STRAIGHT ROAD.

Saint Augustine

AD 354–430, Roman Christian Theologian, Bishop

BEING MISERABLE IS A HABIT; BEING HAPPY IS A HABIT; AND THE CHOICE IS YOURS.

Tom Hopkins

American Author, Sales Trainer

REALIZE THAT TRUE HAPPINESS LIES WITHIN YOU. WASTE NO TIME AND EFFORT SEARCHING FOR THE PEACE AND CONTENTMENT AND JOY IN THE WORLD OUTSIDE. REMEMBER THAT THERE IS NO HAPPINESS IN HAVING OR GETTING, BUT ONLY IN GIVING. REACH OUT. SHARE. SMILE. HUG. HAPPINESS IS A PERFUME YOU CANNOT POUR ON OTHERS WITHOUT GETTING A FEW DROPS ON YOURSELF.

Og Mandino

1923–1996, American Essayist, Psychologist

THERE IS NO SADDER SIGHT THAN A YOUNG PESSIMIST.

Mark Twain

1835–1910, American Humorist, Writer, Lecturer

THERE IS NO FUTURE IN ANY JOB. THE FUTURE LIES IN THE MAN WHO HOLDS THE JOB.

George Crane

PEOPLE OFTEN SAY THAT THIS OR THAT PERSON HAS NOT YET FOUND HIMSELF. BUT THE SELF IS NOT SOMETHING ONE FINDS, IT IS SOMETHING ONE CREATES.

Thomas Szasz

b. 1920, Hungarian-born Psychiatrist, Professor

THEY MAY FORGET WHAT YOU SAID, BUT THEY WILL NEVER FORGET HOW YOU MADE THEM FEEL.

Carl W. Buechner

THE GREATEST DISCOVERY OF ANY GENERATION IS THAT A HUMAN BEING CAN ALTER HIS LIFE BY ALTERING HIS ATTITUDE.

William James

1842—1910, American Philosopher, Psychologist

CHALLENGES CAN BE STEPPING STONES OR STUMBLING BLOCKS. IT IS JUST A MATTER OF HOW YOU VIEW THEM.

Unknown

A POSITIVE ATTITUDE MAY NOT SOLVE ALL YOUR PROBLEMS, BUT IT WILL ANNOY ENOUGH PEOPLE TO MAKE IT WORTH THE EFFORT.

Herm Albright

1876—1944

MAN'S RISE OR FALL, SUCCESS OR FAILURE, HAPPINESS OR UNHAPPINESS DEPENDS ON HIS ATTITUDE . . . A MAN'S ATTITUDE WILL CREATE THE SITUATION HE IMAGINES.

James Allen

1855–1942, New Zealander Statesman

WORK IS EITHER FUN OR DRUDGERY. IT DEPENDS ON YOUR ATTITUDE. I LIKE FUN.

Colleen C. Barrett

THERE ARE NO MENIAL JOBS, ONLY MENIAL ATTITUDES.

William John Bennett

IT'S NOT WHAT HAPPENS TO YOU, BUT HOW YOU REACT TO IT THAT MATTERS.

Epictetus

AD 55–c. 135, Greek Philosopher

WIN AS IF YOU WERE USED TO IT, LOSE AS IF YOU ENJOYED IT FOR A CHANGE.

Golnik Eric

EVENTS WILL TAKE THEIR COURSE, IT IS NO GOOD OF BEING ANGRY AT THEM; HE IS HAPPIEST WHO WISELY TURNS THEM TO THE BEST ACCOUNT.

Euripides

480–406 BC, Greek Tragic Poet

IF THE MIND OF MAN CAN BELIEVE, THE MIND OF MAN CAN ACHIEVE.

Napoleon Hill

1883–1970, American Speaker, Motivational Writer

ABILITY IS WHAT YOU'RE CAPABLE OF DOING. MOTIVATION DETERMINES WHAT YOU DO. ATTITUDE DETERMINES HOW WELL YOU DO IT.

Lou Holtz

b. 1937, American Football Coach

KEEP YOUR FACE TO THE SUNSHINE AND YOU CANNOT SEE THE SHADOW.

Helen Keller

1880—1968, American Author, Educator

WE WOULD ACCOMPLISH MANY MORE THINGS IF WE DID NOT THINK OF THEM AS IMPOSSIBLE.

Chrétien Malesherbes

1721—1794, French Minister of State

SELF-IMAGE SETS THE BOUNDARIES OF INDIVIDUAL ACCOMPLISHMENT.

Maxwell Maltz

1927—2003, American Plastic Surgeon, Motivational Author

TAKE THE ATTITUDE OF A STUDENT: NEVER BE TOO BIG TO ASK QUESTIONS; NEVER KNOW TOO MUCH TO LEARN SOMETHING NEW.

Og Mandino

1923—1996, American Essayist, Psychologist

MORALE IS A STATE OF MIND. IT IS STEADFASTNESS AND COURAGE AND HOPE.

George Marshall

1880–1959, American General, Statesman

A GREAT ATTITUDE DOES MUCH MORE THAN TURN ON THE LIGHTS IN OUR WORLDS; IT SEEMS TO MAGICALLY CONNECT US TO ALL SORTS OF SERENDIPITOUS OPPORTUNITIES THAT WERE SOMEHOW ABSENT BEFORE THE CHANGE.

Earl Nightingale

1921–1989, American Motivational Author

ANY FACT FACING US IS NOT AS IMPORTANT AS OUR ATTITUDE TOWARD IT, FOR THAT DETERMINES OUR SUCCESS OR FAILURE. THE WAY YOU THINK ABOUT A FACT MAY DEFEAT YOU BEFORE YOU EVER DO ANYTHING ABOUT IT. YOU ARE OVERCOME BY THE FACT BECAUSE YOU THINK YOU ARE.

Norman Vincent Peale

1898–1993, American Protestant Clergyman, Writer

IT'S EASY TO LET LIFE DETERIORATE INTO MAKING A LIVING
INSTEAD OF MAKING A LIFE. IT'S NOT THE HOURS YOU PUT IN,
BUT WHAT YOU PUT INTO THE HOURS THAT COUNT. LEARN TO
EXPRESS RATHER THAN IMPRESS. EXPRESSING EVOKES A
"ME TOO" ATTITUDE WHILE IMPRESSING EVOKES A
"SO WHAT" ATTITUDE.

Jim Rohn

American Motivational Speaker, Author

LIFE IS TEN PERCENT WHAT HAPPENS TO YOU
AND NINETY PERCENT HOW
YOU RESPOND TO IT.

Lou Holtz

b. 1937, American Football Coach

THERE ARE ONLY 3 COLORS, 10 DIGITS, AND 7 NOTES;
ITS WHAT WE DO WITH THEM THAT'S IMPORTANT.

Ruth Ross

WE LOST BECAUSE WE TOLD OURSELVES WE LOST.

Leo Tolstoy

1828–1910, Russian Author

ATTITUDE IS MORE IMPORTANT THAN THE PAST, THAN
EDUCATION, THAN MONEY, THAN CIRCUMSTANCES, THAN
WHAT PEOPLE DO OR SAY. IT IS MORE IMPORTANT
THAN APPEARANCE, GIFTEDNESS, OR SKILL.

Charles Swindoll

b. 1934, American Writer, Clergyman

WHO COULD WIN AT THE TOP LEVEL IN ANYTHING TODAY
AND DIDN'T HAVE THE RIGHT ATTITUDE, DIDN'T GIVE IT
EVERYTHING HE HAD, AT LEAST WHILE HE WAS DOING IT;
WASN'T PREPARED AND DIDN'T HAVE THE WHOLE
PROGRAM WORKED OUT.

Ted Turner

b. 1938, American Entrepreneur

LEADERSHIP

WINSTON CHURCHILL, one of the most
important leaders and statesman of the twentieth century, represented
freedom and democracy in a world at war against tyranny. In World War
II he stood alone, leading England against Nazi Germany and Fascist Italy
before the United States was brought into the war on December 7, 1941.

Churchill's background was one of wealth and nobility, but he was not
considered to be a remarkable or accomplished young man. He served
in Parliament, on and off starting in 1901, and in several cabinet posi-
tions. As the political head of the Royal Navy, he failed in his strategy
against Germany in World War I and, as a result, he resigned his position.

Twenty-five years later, Churchill was the right man at the right time to
lead England in World War II. He was the one man who had taken a
strong position against Hitler and Nazi Germany. As a result he was
installed by Parliament as the prime minister. He was the one to warn
England and the free world about the threat from Nazi Germany that
had been ignored.

Churchill's political past was spotty and he had a history of some political and military misjudgments but, in his key role as prime minister, his leadership was essential in defeating Germany. His stubborn refusal to accept an early peace proposal from Hitler, a man that he knew could not be trusted, led to Nazi Germany's total defeat.

The British people resisted constant bombing and rocket attacks and always looked to Churchill for leadership and inspiration.

COURAGE IS THE FIRST OF HUMAN QUALITIES BECAUSE IT IS THE QUALITY WHICH GUARANTEES ALL OTHERS.
Winston Churchill

LEADERSHIP IS THE WILLINGNESS TO ACCEPT RESPONSIBILITY FOR RESULTS.

Brian Tracy

Canadian-born American Author, Business Coach, Motivational Speaker

LITTLE MINDS ATTAIN AND ARE SUBDUED BY MISFORTUNE; BUT GREAT MINDS RISE ABOVE THEM.

Washington Irving

1783–1859, American Writer

BE CAREFUL WHAT YOU PRETEND TO BE BECAUSE YOU ARE WHAT YOU PRETEND TO BE.

Kurt Vonnegut

b. 1922, American Writer

LEADERSHIP IS THE SPECIAL QUALITY WHICH ENABLES PEOPLE TO STAND UP AND PULL THE REST OF US OVER THE HORIZON.

James L. Fisher

THE WORLD HAS A HABIT OF MAKING ROOM FOR THE MAN WHOSE ACTIONS SHOW THAT HE KNOWS WHERE HE IS GOING.

Napoleon Hill

1883–1970, American Speaker, Motivational Writer

A PERSON WHO WALKS IN ANOTHER'S TRACK LEAVES NO FOOTPRINTS.

Unknown

A LEADER IS SOMEONE WHO HELPS IMPROVE THE LIVES OF OTHER PEOPLE OR IMPROVES THE SYSTEM THEY LIVE UNDER.

Sam Ervin

1896–1985, American Senator

LEADERSHIP IS PRACTICED NOT SO MUCH IN WORDS AS IN ATTITUDE AND IN ACTIONS.

Harold S. Geneen

1910–1997, American Businessman

NEARLY ALL MEN CAN STAND ADVERSITY, BUT IF YOU WANT TO TEST A MAN'S CHARACTER, GIVE HIM POWER.

Abraham Lincoln

1809–1865, Sixteenth President of the U.S.

WASTE OF TIME IS THE MOST EXTRAVAGANT AND COSTLY OF ALL EXPENSES.

Unknown

THE FIRST THING A GREAT PERSON DOES, IS MAKE US REALIZE THE INSIGNIFICANCE OF CIRCUMSTANCE.

Ralph Waldo Emerson

1803–1882, American Poet, Essayist

ALONE WE CAN DO SO LITTLE, TOGETHER WE CAN DO SO MUCH.

Helen Keller

1880–1968, American Author, Educator

THERE IS ALWAYS ROOM AT THE TOP.
Daniel Webster
1782–1852, American Statesman

DO NOT GO WHERE THE PATH MAY LEAD, GO INSTEAD WHERE THERE IS NO PATH AND THEN LEAVE A TRAIL.
Ralph Waldo Emerson
1803–1882, American Poet, Essayist

I DON'T BELIEVE IN JUST ORDERING PEOPLE TO DO THINGS. YOU HAVE TO SORT OF GRAB AN OAR AND ROW WITH THEM.
Harold S. Geneen
1910–1997, American Businessman

THERE CAN ONLY BE ONE MAXIM: FULL STEAM AHEAD.
Winston Churchill
1874–1965, British Statesman, Prime Minister

LEADERSHIP IS NOT MAGNETIC PERSONALITY—THAT CAN
JUST AS WELL BE A GLIB TONGUE. IT IS NOT MAKING
FRIENDS AND INFLUENCING PEOPLE—THAT IS FLATTERY.
LEADERSHIP IS LIFTING A PERSON'S VISION TO HIGHER
SIGHTS, THE RAISING OF A PERSON'S PERFORMANCE TO A
HIGHER STANDARD, THE BUILDING OF A PERSONALITY
BEYOND ITS NORMAL LIMITATIONS.

Peter F. Drucker

b. 1909, American Educator, Writer

DISCOVERY OF A SOLUTION CONSISTS OF LOOKING AT THE SAME
THING AS EVERYONE ELSE AND THINKING SOMETHING
DIFFERENT.

Albert Szent-Gyorgyi

1893–1986, Hungarian Biochemist

ONE SECRET OF LEADERSHIP IS THAT THE MIND OF A LEADER
NEVER TURNS OFF. LEADERS, EVEN WHEN THEY ARE SIGHT-
SEERS OR SPECTATORS, ARE ACTIVE; NOT PASSIVE OBSERVERS.

James Humes

IT IS NOT BY MUSCLE, SPEED OR PHYSICAL DEXTERITY THAT GREAT THINGS ARE ACHIEVED, BUT BY REFLECTION, FORCE OF CHARACTER, AND JUDGMENT; IN THESE QUALITIES OLD AGE IS USUALLY NOT ONLY NOT POORER, BUT IT IS EVEN RICHER.

Marcus Tullius Cicero

106–43 BC, Roman Lawyer, Writer, Scholar, Statesman

IT IS THE MARK OF AN EDUCATED MIND TO BE ABLE TO ENTER-TAIN A THOUGHT WITHOUT ACCEPTING IT.

Aristotle

384–322 BC, Greek Philosopher, Scientist, Physician

YOU CAN SUCCESSFULLY FORCE PEOPLE TO FOLLOW A CERTAIN COURSE, BUT YOU CANNOT FORCE THEM TO UNDERSTAND IT.

Confucius

551–479 BC, Chinese Teacher, Philosopher, Political Theorist

IT IS IMPOSSIBLE TO WIN THE RACE UNLESS YOU VENTURE TO RUN, IMPOSSIBLE TO WIN THE VICTORY UNLESS YOU DARE TO BATTLE.

Richard M. DeVos

DON'T FOLLOW TRENDS, START TRENDS.

Frank Capra

1897–1991, Italian-born American Film Director

LEADERSHIP IS THE WISE USE OF POWER. POWER IS THE CAPACITY TO TRANSLATE INTENTION INTO REALITY AND SUSTAIN IT.

Warren G. Bennis

American Writer, Lecturer, Professor

BY THREE METHODS WE MAY LEARN WISDOM: FIRST, BY REFLECTION, WHICH IS NOBLEST; SECOND, BY IMITATION, WHICH IS EASIEST; AND THIRD BY EXPERIENCE, WHICH IS THE BITTEREST.

Confucius

551–479 BC, Chinese Teacher, Philosopher, Political Theorist

THERE ARE NO OFFICE HOURS FOR LEADERS.

Cardinal James Gibbons

LIFE IS NO BRIEF CANDLE TO ME. IT IS A SORT OF SPLENDID
TORCH WHICH I HAVE GOT A HOLD OF FOR THE MOMENT, AND I
WANT TO MAKE IT BURN AS BRIGHTLY AS POSSIBLE BEFORE
HANDING IT ON TO FUTURE GENERATIONS.

George Bernard Shaw

1856–1950, Irish Literary Critic, Playwright, Essayist

IF WE WAIT FOR THE MOMENT WHEN EVERYTHING,
ABSOLUTELY EVERYTHING IS READY, WE
SHALL NEVER BEGIN.

Ivan Turgenev

1818–1883, Russian Author

THE VERY ESSENCE OF LEADERSHIP IS THAT YOU
HAVE TO HAVE VISION. YOU CAN'T BLOW AN
UNCERTAIN TRUMPET.

Theodore M. Hesburgh

b. 1917, American Clergyman, Former President of University of Notre Dame

SUCCESS ON ANY MAJOR SCALE REQUIRES YOU TO ACCEPT
RESPONSIBILITY . . . IN THE FINAL ANALYSIS,
THE ONE QUALITY THAT ALL SUCCESSFUL
PEOPLE HAVE . . . IS THE ABILITY TO
TAKE RESPONSIBILITY.

Michael Korda

THE LEADER SEEKS TO COMMUNICATE HIS VISION TO HIS
FOLLOWERS. HE CAPTURES THEIR ATTENTION WITH HIS
OPTIMISTIC INTUITION OF POSSIBLE SOLUTIONS TO THEIR
NEEDS. HE INFLUENCES THEM BY THE DYNAMISM
OF HIS FAITH. HE DEMONSTRATES CONFIDENCE
THAT THE CHALLENGE CAN BE MET,
THE NEED RESOLVED, THE CRISIS OVERCOME.

John Haggai

American Clergyman

A GOOD OBJECTIVE OF LEADERSHIP IS TO HELP THOSE WHO
ARE DOING POORLY TO DO WELL AND TO HELP THOSE WHO ARE
DOING WELL TO DO EVEN BETTER.

Jim Rohn

American Motivational Speaker, Author

IF YOU DON'T HAVE THE TIME TO DO IT RIGHT,
YOU MUST HAVE THE TIME TO DO IT OVER.

Unknown

YOU DO NOT LEAD BY HITTING PEOPLE OVER THE HEAD—
THAT'S ASSAULT, NOT LEADERSHIP.

Dwight D. Eisenhower

1890–1969, Thirty-fourth President of the U.S.

IT IS BETTER TO BELIEVE THAN TO DISBELIEVE, IN SO DOING YOU BRING EVERYTHING TO THE REALM OF POSSIBILITY.

Albert Einstein

1879–1955, German-born American Physicist

WHENEVER YOU DO A THING, ACT AS IF ALL THE WORLD WERE WATCHING.

Thomas Jefferson

1762–1826, Third President of the U.S.

WISE LEADERS GENERALLY HAVE WISE COUNSELORS BECAUSE IT TAKES A WISE PERSON THEMSELVES TO DISTINGUISH THEM.

Diogenes of Sinope

412–323 BC, Greek Philosopher

WHO HAS NOT SERVED CANNOT COMMAND.

John Florio

1553–1625, English Translator, Writer

**I SUPPOSE LEADERSHIP AT ONE TIME MEANT MUSCLES;
BUT TODAY IT MEANS GETTING ALONG WITH PEOPLE.**

Mahatma Gandhi

1869–1948, Indian Philosopher

**SHOW CLASS, HAVE PRIDE, AND DISPLAY CHARACTER.
IF YOU DO, WINNING TAKES CARE OF ITSELF.**

Paul "Bear" Bryant

1913–1983, American Football Coach

**A LEADER IS A PERSON YOU WILL FOLLOW
TO A PLACE YOU WOULDN'T
GO BY YOURSELF.**

Joel A. Barker

**DON'T MEASURE YOURSELF BY WHAT YOU HAVE
ACCOMPLISHED, BUT BY WHAT YOU SHOULD HAVE
ACCOMPLISHED WITH YOUR ABILITY.**

Unknown

OBSTACLES DON'T HAVE TO STOP YOU. IF YOU RUN INTO A WALL, DON'T TURN AROUND AND GIVE UP. FIGURE OUT HOW TO CLIMB IT, GO THROUGH IT, OR WORK AROUND IT.

Michael Jordan

b. 1963, American Basketball Player

LEADERSHIP SHOULD BE BORN OUT OF THE UNDERSTANDING OF THE NEEDS OF THOSE WHO WOULD BE AFFECTED BY IT.

Marian Anderson

1902–1993, American Singer

WHEN YOU CEASE TO DREAM YOU CEASE TO LIVE.

Malcolm S. Forbes

1917–1990, American Publisher, Entrepreneur

MEN WILLINGLY BELIEVE WHAT THEY WISH.

Julius Caesar

100–44 BC, Roman General, Statesman, Emperor of Rome

THE CHIEF EXECUTIVE WHO KNOWS HIS STRENGTHS
AND WEAKNESSES AS A LEADER IS LIKELY TO BE FAR MORE
EFFECTIVE THAN THE ONE WHO REMAINS BLIND TO THEM.
HE ALSO IS ON THE ROAD TO HUMILITY—THAT
PRICELESS ATTITUDE OF OPENNESS TO LIFE
THAT CAN HELP A MANAGER ABSORB MISTAKES,
FAILURES, OR PERSONAL SHORTCOMINGS.

John Adair

BEHOLD THE TURTLE. HE MAKES PROGRESS ONLY
WHEN HE STICKS HIS NECK OUT.

James B. Conant

1893–1978, American Educator, Scientist

I WAS NOT THE LION, BUT IT FELL TO ME TO GIVE
THE LION'S ROAR.

Winston Churchill

1874–1965, British Statesman, Prime Minister

IF YOU DON'T RUN YOUR OWN LIFE,
SOMEBODY ELSE WILL.

John Atkinson

A GOOD LEADER TAKES A LITTLE MORE THAN HIS SHARE OF
THE BLAME, A LITTLE LESS THAN HIS SHARE
OF THE CREDIT.

Arnold H. Glasgow

THE ONLY LIMITS ARE, AS ALWAYS,
THOSE OF VISION.

James Broughton

1913–1999, American Filmmaker, Poet, Playwright

LEADERS CREATE AN ENVIRONMENT IN WHICH EVERYONE
HAS THE OPPORTUNITY TO DO WORK THAT MATCHES
HIS POTENTIAL CAPABILITY AND FOR WHICH AN
EQUITABLE DIFFERENTIAL
REWARD IS PROVIDED.

Elliott Jaques

1917–2003, Canadian-born Psychologist, Social Analyst

AVERAGE PEOPLE LOOK FOR WAYS OF
GETTING AWAY WITH IT; SUCCESSFUL PEOPLE
LOOK FOR WAYS OF GETTING ON WITH IT.

Jim Rohn

American Motivational Speaker, Author

SKILL IN THE ART OF COMMUNICATION IS CRUCIAL TO A
LEADER'S SUCCESS. HE CAN ACCOMPLISH NOTHING
UNLESS HE CAN COMMUNICATE EFFECTIVELY.

Norman Allen

A BOSS CREATES FEAR, A LEADER CONFIDENCE. A BOSS FIXES
BLAME, A LEADER CORRECTS MISTAKES. A BOSS KNOWS ALL, A
LEADER ASKS QUESTIONS. A BOSS MAKES WORK DRUDGERY, A
LEADER MAKES IT INTERESTING. A BOSS IS INTERESTED IN HIM-
SELF OR HERSELF, A LEADER IS INTERESTED IN THE GROUP.

Russell H. Ewing

NO MAN CAN PERSUADE PEOPLE TO DO WHAT
HE WANTS THEM TO DO UNLESS HE GENUINELY LIKES PEOPLE
AND BELIEVES THAT WHAT HE WANTS THEM TO DO IS TO THEIR
OWN ADVANTAGE.

Bruce Barton

1886–1967, American Congressman

IF THERE IS ANY ONE AXIOM THAT I HAVE TRIED TO LIVE UP TO
IN ATTEMPTING TO BECOME SUCCESSFUL IN BUSINESS, IT IS
THE FACT THAT I HAVE TRIED TO SURROUND MYSELF WITH
ASSOCIATES THAT KNOW MORE ABOUT BUSINESS THAN I DO.
THIS POLICY HAS ALWAYS BEEN VERY SUCCESSFUL AND IS
STILL WORKING FOR ME.

Monte L. Bean

SIX TRAITS OF EFFECTIVE LEADERS:
1. MAKE OTHERS FEEL IMPORTANT 2. PROMOTE A VISION
3. FOLLOW THE GOLDEN RULE 4. ADMIT MISTAKES
5. CRITICIZE OTHERS ONLY IN PRIVATE 6. STAY CLOSE TO
THE ACTION. EXAMPLE HAS MORE FOLLOWERS THAN REASON.
WE UNCONSCIOUSLY IMITATE WHAT PLEASES US, AND
APPROXIMATE TO THE CHARACTERS WE MOST ADMIRE.

John Christian Bovee

THE MAN WHO FOLLOWS A CROWD WILL NEVER
BE FOLLOWED BY A CROWD.

R. S. Donnell

LEADERSHIP IS THE ART OF GETTING SOMEONE ELSE
TO DO SOMETHING YOU WANT DONE
BECAUSE HE WANTS TO DO IT.

Dwight D. Eisenhower

1890–1969, Thirty-fourth President of the U.S.

RECOGNITION IS THE GREATEST
MOTIVATOR.

Gerard C. Eakedale

PERSEVERANCE

JACKIE ROBINSON, the first African-American player in major league baseball, carried the tremendous burden of having to perform as a star and resist the prejudice and segregation he faced daily.

In 1947 Robinson played his first major league game and became a target of hate for many players and fans. It was a hostile environment with many opposing players, and even some of Robinson's own teammates, initially opposed to his presence. The opposing pitchers threw at him and many of the fans mocked him. Few men could have endured this punishment without lashing back.

Before he began his career, Robinson had promised Branch Rickey, president of the Dodgers, that he could and would persevere through all of the hatred and bigotry. At the end of the year Robinson was voted Rookie of the Year and two years later, in 1949, he was voted MVP of the league.

Robinson had carried the hopes of every African-American baseball player on his shoulders and opened the doors for integration. After ten years with the Dodgers, he retired and continued to persevere to fight injustice and be a spokesman for equality.

Jackie Robinson was elected to the National Baseball Hall of Fame in 1962 and died at the age of fifty-two in 1972.

WE ASK FOR NOTHING SPECIAL. WE ASK ONLY TO BE PERMITTED TO LIVE AS YOU LIVE, AND AS OUR NATION'S CONSTITUTION PROVIDES.

Jackie Robinson

THE HARDER YOU WORK, THE HARDER
IT IS TO SURRENDER.

Bill Dooley

THE WORLD ISN'T INTERESTED IN THE STORMS YOU
ENCOUNTERED, BUT WHETHER OR NOT YOU
BROUGHT IN THE SHIP.

Raul Armesto

IF YOU'VE REALLY DONE YOUR BEST, YOU PROBABLY
WON'T HAVE TO THINK UP AN EXCUSE
FOR NOT DOING BETTER.

Unknown

THE HIGHEST REWARD FOR A MAN'S TOIL IS NOT
WHAT HE GETS FOR IT BUT WHAT HE
BECOMES BY IT.

John Ruskin

1819–1900, English Writer, Art Critic, Architecture Critic

SOME MEN GIVE UP THEIR DESIGNS WHEN THEY
HAVE ALMOST REACHED THE GOAL, WHILE OTHERS,
ON THE CONTRARY, OBTAIN A VICTORY BY EXERTING,
AT THE LAST MOMENT, MORE VIGOROUS EFFORTS
THAN EVER BEFORE.

Herodotus

484–c. 430 BC, Greek Author

IT IS A ROUGH ROAD THAT LEADS
TO THE HEIGHTS OF
GREATNESS.

Lucius Annaeus Seneca

3 BC–AD 65, Roman Philosopher

THE GREATER THE OBSTACLE, THE MORE GLORY
IN OVERCOMING IT.

Molière

1622–1673, French Actor, Playwright, Writer

OUR GREATEST GLORY IS NOT IN NEVER FALLING, BUT RISING EVERY TIME WE FALL.

Confucius

551–479 BC, Chinese Teacher, Philosopher, Political Theorist

I DO THE VERY BEST I KNOW HOW—THE VERY BEST I CAN; AND I MEAN TO KEEP ON DOING SO UNTIL THE END.

Abraham Lincoln

1809–1865, Sixteenth President of the U.S.

THE PRICE OF SUCCESS IS PERSEVERANCE. THE PRICE OF FAILURE IS MUCH CHEAPER.

Unknown

I THINK AND THINK FOR MONTHS AND YEARS. NINETY-NINE TIMES, THE CONCLUSION IS FALSE. THE HUNDREDTH TIME I AM RIGHT.

Albert Einstein

1879–1955, German-born American Physicist

EVERY MAN DIES. NOT EVERY MAN LIVES. THE ONLY LIMITS TO THE POSSIBILITIES IN YOUR LIFE TOMORROW ARE THE "BUTS" YOU USE TODAY.

Les Brown

1912—2001, American Songwriter

BASEBALL IS THE ONLY FIELD OF ENDEAVOR WHERE A MAN CAN SUCCEED THREE TIMES OUT OF 10 AND BE CONSIDERED A GOOD PERFORMER.

Ted Williams

1918—2002, American Baseball Player

OPPORTUNITY RARELY KNOCKS ON YOUR DOOR. KNOCK RATHER ON OPPORTUNITY'S DOOR IF YOU ARDENTLY WISH TO ENTER.

B. C. Forbes

1880—1954, Scottish-born American Editor, Founder of Forbes magazine

I MIGHT HAVE BEEN BORN IN A HOVEL BUT I DETERMINED TO TRAVEL WITH THE WIND AND THE STARS.

Jacqueline Cochran

NEARLY EVERY MAN WHO DEVELOPS AN IDEA
WORKS AT IT UP TO THE POINT WHERE
IT LOOKS IMPOSSIBLE, AND THEN
GETS DISCOURAGED. THAT'S NOT THE
PLACE TO BECOME DISCOURAGED.

Thomas A. Edison

1847–1931, American Inventor, Entrepreneur, Founder of GE

WHEN THE MORNING'S FRESHNESS HAS BEEN REPLACED
BY THE WEARINESS OF MIDDAY, WHEN THE LEG MUSCLES
GIVE UNDER THE STRAIN, THE CLIMB SEEMS ENDLESS,
AND SUDDENLY NOTHING WILL GO QUITE
AS YOU WISH—IT IS THEN THAT
YOU MUST NOT HESITATE.

Dag Hammarskjold

1905–1961, Swedish Statesman

NOTHING IN THE WORLD CAN TAKE THE PLACE OF
PERSISTENCE. TALENT WILL NOT; NOTHING IS MORE
COMMON THAN UNSUCCESSFUL MEN WITH TALENT.
GENIUS WILL NOT; UNREWARDED GENIUS IS
ALMOST A PROVERB. EDUCATION WILL NOT; THE
WORLD IS FULL OF EDUCATED DERELICTS.
PERSISTENCE AND DETERMINATION
ALONE ARE OMNIPOTENT.

Calvin Coolidge

1872–1933, Thirtieth President of the U.S.

THE REWARDS FOR THOSE WHO PERSEVERE FAR
EXCEED THE PAIN THAT MUST PRECEDE THE VICTORY.

Ted Engstrom

YOU WILL FIND THAT, WHATEVER YOU ARE DOING IN LIFE,
OBSTACLES DON'T MATTER VERY MUCH. PAIN OR OTHER
CIRCUMSTANCES CAN BE THERE, BUT IF YOU WANT TO DO
A JOB BAD ENOUGH, YOU'LL FIND A WAY.

Jack Youngblood

YOU'VE GOT TO SAY, "I THINK THAT IF I KEEP WORKING
AT THIS AND WANT IT BADLY ENOUGH,
I CAN HAVE IT." IT'S CALLED
PERSEVERANCE.

Lee Iacocca

b. 1924, American Businessman, Former CEO of Chrysler

GENIUS IS ONE PERCENT INSPIRATION AND
NINETY-NINE PERCENT
PERSPIRATION.

Thomas A. Edison

1847–1931, American Inventor, Entrepreneur, Founder of GE

IT'S THE CONSTANT AND DETERMINED EFFORT THAT
BREAKS DOWN ALL RESISTANCE, SWEEPS AWAY
ALL OBSTACLES.
Claude M. Bristol

A GREAT PLEASURE IN LIFE IS DOING WHAT
PEOPLE SAY YOU CANNOT DO.
Walter Gagehot

ENTREPRENEURS AVERAGE 3.8 FAILURES BEFORE FINAL
SUCCESS. WHAT SETS THE SUCCESSFUL ONES APART IS
THEIR AMAZING PERSISTENCE. THERE ARE A LOT OF
PEOPLE OUT THERE WITH GOOD AND MARKETABLE
IDEAS, BUT PURE ENTREPRENEURIAL TYPES
ALMOST NEVER ACCEPT DEFEAT.
Lisa M. Amos

NO MAN IS EVER WHIPPED UNTIL HE QUITS IN HIS OWN MIND.
Napoleon Hill
1883–1970, American Speaker, Motivational Writer

ANY MAN CAN WORK WHEN EVERY STROKE OF HIS HANDS
BRINGS DOWN THE FRUIT RATTLING FROM THE TREE . . . BUT
TO LABOR IN SEASON AND OUT OF SEASON, UNDER EVERY
DISCOURAGEMENT . . . THAT REQUIRES A HEROISM
WHICH IS TRANSCENDENT.

Henry Ward Beecher

1813–1887, American Congregational Minister, Author

I NEVER FAILED ONCE. IT JUST HAPPENED TO BE A
20001-STEP PROCESS.

Thomas A. Edison

1847–1931, American Inventor, Entrepreneur, Founder of GE

WHEN YOU GET INTO A TIGHT PLACE, AND EVERYTHING
GOES AGAINST YOU, TILL IT SEEMS AS THOUGH YOU
COULD NOT HOLD ON A MOMENT LONGER, NEVER
GIVE UP THEN—FOR THAT IS JUST THE PLACE
AND TIME THAT THE TIDE WILL TURN.

Harriet Beecher Stowe

1811–1896, American Writer, Philanthropist

PERSEVERANCE IS FAILING NINETEEN TIMES AND SUCCEEDING THE TWENTIETH.

Julie Andrews

b. 1935, British Actress, Singer

AERODYNAMICALLY THE BUMBLE BEE SHOULD NOT BE ABLE TO FLY, BUT THE BUMBLE BEE DOESN'T KNOW IT, SO IT GOES ON FLYING ANYWAY.

Mary Kay Ash

1915–2001, American Businesswoman, Founder of Mary Kay Cosmetics

LET ME TELL YOU THE SECRET THAT HAS LED ME TO MY GOAL: MY STRENGTH LIES SOLELY IN MY TENACITY.

Louis Pasteur

1822–1895, French Chemist

IF I HAD TO SELECT ONE QUALITY, ONE PERSONAL CHARACTER-ISTIC THAT I REGARD AS BEING MOST HIGHLY CORRELATED WITH SUCCESS, WHATEVER THE FIELD, I WOULD PICK THE TRAIT OF PERSISTENCE. DETERMINATION. THE WILL TO ENDURE TO THE END, TO GET KNOCKED DOWN SEVENTY TIMES AND GET UP OFF THE FLOOR SAYING, "HERE COMES NUMBER SEVENTY-ONE!"

Richard M. DeVos

THE MOST REWARDING THINGS YOU DO IN LIFE ARE OFTEN THE ONES THAT LOOK LIKE THEY CANNOT BE DONE.

Arnold Palmer

b. 1929, American Golfer

PERSEVERANCE IS NOT A LONG RACE; IT IS MANY SHORT RACES ONE AFTER ANOTHER.

Walter Elliot

1842–1928, American Catholic Priest, Writer

WITH ORDINARY TALENTS AND EXTRAORDINARY PERSEVERANCE, ALL THINGS ARE ATTAINABLE.

Sir Thomas Fowell Buxton

ALL RISING TO A GREAT PLACE IS BY A WINDING STAIR.

Francis Bacon

1561–1626, English Lawyer, Philosopher

I DO NOT THINK THERE IS ANY OTHER QUALITY SO ESSENTIAL TO SUCCESS OF ANY KIND AS THE QUALITY OF PERSEVERANCE. IT OVERCOMES ALMOST EVERYTHING, EVEN NATURE.

John D. Rockefeller

1839–1937, American Industrialist, Philanthropist, Founder of Exxon

WHAT THE POWER IS I CANNOT SAY; ALL I KNOW IS THAT IT EXISTS AND IT BECOMES AVAILABLE ONLY WHEN A MAN IS IN THAT STATE OF MIND IN WHICH HE KNOWS EXACTLY WHAT HE WANTS AND IS FULLY DETERMINED NOT TO QUIT UNTIL HE FINDS IT.

Alexander Graham Bell

1847–1922, Scottish-born American Inventor, Educator

PERSEVERE AND GET IT DONE.

George E. Allen

1922–1990, American Football Coach

MOST OF THE IMPORTANT THINGS IN THE WORLD HAVE BEEN ACCOMPLISHED BY PEOPLE WHO HAVE KEPT ON TRYING WHEN THERE SEEMED TO BE NO HELP AT ALL.

Dale Carnegie

1888–1955, American Lecturer, Author

HISTORY HAS DEMONSTRATED THAT THE MOST NOTABLE
WINNERS USUALLY ENCOUNTERED HEARTBREAKING OBSTACLES
BEFORE THEY TRIUMPHED. THEY WON BECAUSE THEY REFUSED
TO BECOME DISCOURAGED BY THEIR DEFEATS.

B. C. Forbes

1880–1954, Scottish-born American Editor, Founder of Forbes *magazine*

I HAVE MISSED MORE THAN 9,000 SHOTS IN MY CAREER. I HAVE
LOST ALMOST 300 GAMES. ON 26 OCCASIONS I HAVE BEEN
ENTRUSTED TO TAKE THE GAME-WINNING SHOT . . . AND I
MISSED. I HAVE FAILED OVER AND OVER AND OVER AGAIN IN MY
LIFE. AND THAT'S PRECISELY WHY I SUCCEED.

Michael Jordan

b. 1963, American Basketball Player

ALL THE SUGAR WAS IN THE
BOTTOM OF THE CUP.

Julia Ward Howe

MOST PEOPLE GIVE UP JUST WHEN THEY'RE ABOUT TO ACHIEVE
SUCCESS. THEY GIVE UP ON THE ONE-FOOT LINE. THEY GIVE UP
AT THE LAST MINUTE OF THE GAME ONE FOOT FROM A WINNING
TOUCHDOWN.

H. Ross Perot

b. 1930, American Businessman

I WANT TO BE THOROUGHLY USED UP WHEN I DIE, FOR THE HARDER I WORK THE MORE I LIVE. I REJOICE IN LIFE FOR ITS OWN SAKE.

George Bernard Shaw

1856–1950, Irish Literary Critic, Playwright, Essayist

PLAY THE GAME FOR MORE THAN YOU CAN AFFORD TO LOSE . . . ONLY THEN WILL YOU LEARN THE GAME.

Winston Churchill

1874–1965, British Statesman, Prime Minister

EVERY GREAT LEAP FORWARD IN YOUR LIFE COMES AFTER YOU HAVE MADE A CLEAR DECISION OF SOME KIND.

Brian Tracy

Canadian-born American Author, Business Coach, Motivational Speaker

WHATEVER YOU DO, YOU NEED COURAGE. WHATEVER COURSE YOU DECIDE UPON, THERE IS ALWAYS SOMEONE TO TELL YOU THAT YOU ARE WRONG. THERE ARE ALWAYS DIFFICULTIES ARISING THAT TEMPT YOU TO BELIEVE YOUR CRITICS ARE RIGHT. TO MAP OUT A COURSE OF ACTION AND FOLLOW IT TO AN END REQUIRES SOME OF THE SAME COURAGE THAT A SOLDIER NEEDS. PEACE HAS ITS VICTORIES, BUT IT TAKES BRAVE MEN AND WOMEN TO WIN THEM.

Ralph Waldo Emerson

1803–1882, American Poet, Essayist

PEOPLE OF MEDIOCRE ABILITY SOMETIMES ACHIEVE OUT-STANDING SUCCESS BECAUSE THEY DON'T KNOW WHEN TO QUIT. MOST MEN SUCCEED BECAUSE THEY ARE DETERMINED TO.

George E. Allen

1922–1990, American Football Coach

NEVER GIVE UP. KEEP YOUR THOUGHTS AND YOUR MIND ALWAYS ON THE GOAL.

Tom Bradley

A JUG FILLS DROP BY DROP.

Buddha

563–483 BC, Hindu Prince

PERSISTENT PEOPLE BEGIN THEIR SUCCESS WHERE OTHERS END IN FAILURE.

Edward Eggleston

PATIENCE

HELEN KELLER lost her hearing and her sight when she was nineteen months old from a severe fever, believed to be either scarlet fever or meningitis.

Helen's parents found it difficult to raise her and sought help. Alexander Graham Bell, the inventor of the telephone, referred her parents to an institution that recommended Anne Sullivan as a teacher for Helen.

Anne had lost the majority of her sight by the age of five but, through two operations, she regained enough sight to be able to read normal print.

Months of long, difficult attempts to teach were finally rewarded when Helen realized the association between words and things. Rapid learning that was called astounding and phenomenal followed this breakthrough.

Through a series of teachers and the constant help and companionship of Anne Sullivan, Helen was able to attend and graduate from Radcliffe College, becoming the first deaf and blind person to do so.

Helen began to write but was never really able to learn to speak. Her writings were published and she became well known. She and Anne eventually went on lecture tours, with Anne providing the voice to Helen's views and thoughts.

Helen and Anne did extensive fundraising for the blind. Over the years, Anne became ill and could no longer speak for Helen. Polly Thomson, their secretary, replaced Anne and Helen continued to tour, lecture and raise money for the blind. Anne Sullivan died in 1936 and Polly Thomson died in 1960. Before Helen died in 1968, she was honored many times for her books, and in the creation of a Broadway play and a movie about her and Anne.

Years of patience and hard work gave life real meaning to Helen Keller and contributed greatly to opening up new opportunities for the blind and deaf.

WE CAN DO ANYTHING WE WANT TO DO IF WE STICK TO IT LONG ENOUGH.
Helen Keller

PATIENCE IS THE COMPANION OF WISDOM.

Saint Augustine

354–430, Roman Christian Theologian, Bishop

PATIENCE IS THE MOST NECESSARY QUALITY FOR BUSINESS, MANY A MAN WOULD RATHER YOU HEARD HIS STORY THAN GRANT HIS REQUEST.

Philip Dormer Stanhope Chesterfield

ONLY THOSE WHO HAVE THE PATIENCE TO DO SIMPLE THINGS PERFECTLY WILL ACQUIRE THE SKILL TO DO DIFFICULT THINGS EASILY.

Johann Friedrich von Schiller

THE SECRET OF PATIENCE IS TO DO SOMETHING ELSE IN THE MEANTIME.

Spanish Proverb

IN THE LONG RUN YOU HIT ONLY WHAT YOU AIM AT. THEREFORE, THOUGH YOU SHOULD FAIL IMMEDIATELY, YOU HAD BETTER AIM AT SOMETHING HIGH.

Henry David Thoreau

1817–1862, American Essayist, Poet, Naturalist

A LACK OF PATIENCE IN TRIFLING MATTERS MIGHT LEAD TO THE DISRUPTION OF GREAT PROJECT.

Confucius

551–479 BC, Chinese Teacher, Philosopher, Political Theorist

IF I HAVE EVER MADE ANY VALUABLE DISCOVERIES, IT HAS BEEN OWING MORE TO PATIENT ATTENTION, THAN TO ANY OTHER TALENT.

Isaac Newton

1642–1727, English Mathematician, Physicist

I HAVE LEARNED THE NOVICE CAN OFTEN SEE THINGS THAT THE EXPERT OVERLOOKS. ALL THAT IS NECESSARY IS NOT TO BE AFRAID OF MAKING MISTAKES, OR OF APPEARING NAÏVE.

Abraham Maslow

1908–1970, American Philosopher, Psychologist

**A HANDFUL OF PATIENCE IS WORTH MORE THAN
A BUSHEL OF BRAINS.**

Dutch Proverb

**ONE OF THE MOST VALUABLE LESSONS I LEARNED . . . IS THAT
WE ALL HAVE TO LEARN FROM OUR MISTAKES, AND WE LEARN
FROM THOSE MISTAKES A LOT MORE THAN WE LEARN FROM
THE THINGS WE SUCCEEDED IN DOING.**

Ann Richards

TO KNOW HOW TO WAIT. IT IS THE GREAT SECRET OF SUCCESS.

Joseph De Maistre

**PATIENCE IS BITTER BUT
ITS REWARD IS SWEET.**

Unknown

EVERYTHING COMES TO HIM WHO HUSTLES WHILE HE WAITS.

Thomas A. Edison

1847–1931, American Inventor, Entrepreneur, Founder of GE

PATIENCE AND PERSEVERANCE HAVE A MAGICAL EFFECT BEFORE WHICH DIFFICULTIES DISAPPEAR AND OBSTACLES VANISH.

John Quincy Adams

1767–1848, Sixth President of the U.S.

IT TAKES TIME TO SUCCEED BECAUSE SUCCESS IS MERELY THE NATURAL REWARD OF TAKING TIME TO DO ANYTHING WELL.

Joseph Ross

I BELIEVE I WAS IMPATIENT WITH UNINTELLIGENT PEOPLE FROM THE MOMENT I WAS BORN: A TRAGEDY—FOR I AM MYSELF THREE-PARTS A FOOL.

Patrick Campbell

EXPECT TROUBLE AS AN INEVITABLE PART OF LIFE
AND REPEAT TO YOURSELF THE MOST COMFORTING WORDS
OF ALL: "THIS, TOO, SHALL PASS."

Ann Landers

1918–2002, American Advice Columnist

ALL HUMAN ERRORS ARE IMPATIENCE, A PREMATURE
BREAKING OFF OF METHODICAL PROCEDURE,
AN APPARENT FENCING IN OF WHAT IS
APPARENTLY AT ISSUE.

Franz Kafka

1883–1924, German Writer

HAVE PATIENCE WITH ALL THINGS, BUT CHIEFLY HAVE
PATIENCE WITH YOURSELF. DO NOT LOSE COURAGE IN
CONSIDERING YOUR OWN IMPERFECTIONS BUT
INSTANTLY SET ABOUT REMEDYING THEM—EVERY DAY
BEGIN THE TASK ANEW.

Saint Francis de Sales

IF YOU WANT A RAINBOW, YOU MUST
PUT UP WITH THE RAIN.

Dolly Parton

b. 1946, American Singer

I AM EXTRAORDINARILY PATIENT, PROVIDED I GET MY OWN WAY IN THE END.

Margaret Thatcher

b. 1925, British Politician, Prime Minister

THERE WILL BE A TIME WHEN LOUD-MOUTHED, INCOMPETENT PEOPLE SEEM TO BE GETTING THE BEST OF YOU. WHEN THAT HAPPENS, YOU ONLY HAVE TO BE PATIENT AND WAIT FOR THEM TO SELF-DESTRUCT. IT NEVER FAILS.

Richard Rybolt

GENIUS IS NOTHING BUT A GREATER APTITUDE FOR PATIENCE.

Benjamin Franklin

1706–1790, American Scientist, Publisher, Diplomat

HAPPINESS IS A BUTTERFLY WHICH, WHEN PURSUED, IS ALWAYS BEYOND OUR GRASP, BUT, IF YOU WILL SIT DOWN QUIETLY, MAY ALIGHT UPON YOU.

Nathaniel Hawthorne

1804–1864, American Novelist, Short Story Writer

LEARN THE ART OF PATIENCE. APPLY DISCIPLINE TO YOUR THOUGHTS WHEN THEY BECOME ANXIOUS OVER THE OUTCOME OF A GOAL. IMPATIENCE BREEDS ANXIETY, FEAR, DISCOURAGE-MENT, AND FAILURE. PATIENCE CREATES CONFIDENCE, DECISIVENESS, AND A RATIONAL OUTLOOK, WHICH EVENTUALLY LEADS TO SUCCESS.

Brian Adams

PATIENCE HAS ITS LIMITS. TAKE IT TOO FAR, AND IT'S COWARDICE.

George Jackson

THERE IS A SLOWNESS IN AFFAIRS WHICH RIPENS THEM, AND A SLOWNESS WHICH ROTS THEM.

Joseph Roux

1725–1793, French Artist

LIKE FARMERS WE NEED TO LEARN THAT WE CANNOT SOW AND REAP THE SAME DAY.

Unknown

PATIENCE WILL ACHIEVE MORE THAN FORCE.

Edmund Burke

1729–1797, British Political Writer, Statesman

THE KEY TO EVERYTHING IS PATIENCE. YOU GET THE CHICKEN BY HATCHING THE EGG, NOT BY SMASHING IT OPEN.

Arnold H. Glasgow

IT IS BY ATTEMPTING TO REACH THE TOP IN A SINGLE LEAP THAT SO MUCH MISERY IS PRODUCED IN THE WORLD.

William Cobbett

1762–1835, British Journalist, Reformer

MANAGING

BILL GATES, cofounder of Microsoft with his childhood
friend Paul Allen, is the richest person in the world with 46 billion dollars.

Gates is also a good manager and visionary. Early on, he had a vision of
a tabletop, user-friendly computer and the software that he was interested
in developing.

He is the author of two bestselling business books and is well known for
his philanthropy, having given away billions of dollars to many and
varied organizations and causes.

Gates's management style is innovative, designed to attract and retain the best talent. He brought in Steve Ballmer, a classmate from Harvard, as CEO. Gates knows that it is important to hire the best people and spend large amounts of money on research and development to compete against the other formidable software houses.

Bill Gates's hands-on approach to management has led Microsoft to consistent and profitable growth.

A NERD COULDN'T BE A GOOD MANAGER AND A GOOD LEADER OF A COMPANY.
Bill Gates

REMEMBER THAT LIFE IS NOT MEASURED
IN HOURS BUT IN ACCOMPLISHMENTS.

James A. Pike

YOUR SUCCESS IS MEASURED BY YOUR
ABILITY TO COMPLETE THINGS.

Unknown

SURROUND YOURSELF WITH THE BEST
PEOPLE YOU CAN FIND, DELEGATE AUTHORITY,
AND DON'T INTERFERE.

Ronald Reagan

1911–2004, Fortieth President of the U.S.

THE DIFFERENCE BETWEEN THE IMPOSSIBLE
AND THE POSSIBLE LIES IN A
MAN'S DETERMINATION.

Tommy Lasorda

b. 1927, American Baseball Player, Coach

WE MUST USE TIME AS A TOOL, NOT AS A CRUTCH.

John F. Kennedy

1917–1963, Thirty-fifth President of the U.S.

MOST OF US CAN DO MORE THAN WE THINK WE CAN, BUT WE USUALLY DO LESS THAN WE THINK WE DO.

Unknown

THE ABILITY TO ASK THE RIGHT QUESTION IS MORE THAN HALF THE BATTLE OF FINDING THE ANSWER.

Thomas J. Watson

1874–1956, American Entrepreneur, Founder of IBM

DO NOT CONFUSE MOTION AND PROGRESS. A ROCKING HORSE KEEPS MOVING BUT DOES NOT MAKE ANY PROGRESS.

Alfred A. Montapert

American Motivational Author

MANAGEMENT IS NOTHING MORE THAN MOTIVATING OTHER PEOPLE.

Lee Iacocca

b. 1924, American Businessman, Former CEO of Chrysler

WINNERS ARE ALWAYS LOOKING FOR A WAY TO DEAL WITH THE CHALLENGES THAT THEY FACE, AND LOSERS ARE ALWAYS MAKING EXCUSES TO AVOID DEALING WITH CHALLENGES.

Brian Tracy

Canadian-born American Author, Business Coach, Motivational Speaker

EVERYONE HAS PROBLEMS—THAT'S JUST A FACT OF LIFE. HOWEVER, POSITIVE THINKERS TURN THEIR PROBLEMS INTO OPPORTUNITIES. ARE YOU A POSITIVE THINKER?

Unknown

NOTHING IS A WASTE OF TIME IF YOU USE THE EXPERIENCE WISELY.

Auguste Rodin

1840–1917, French Sculptor

SUCCESS IS THE MAXIMUM UTILIZATION OF THE ABILITY THAT YOU HAVE.

Zig Ziglar

b. 1926, American Motivational Speaker, Author

THE PROBLEM IS NOT THAT THERE ARE PROBLEMS. THE PROBLEM IS EXPECTING OTHERWISE AND THINKING THAT HAVING PROBLEMS IS A PROBLEM.

Theodore Rubin

b. 1923, American Writer, Psychiatrist

HIRE THE BEST. PAY THEM FAIRLY. COMMUNICATE FREQUENTLY. PROVIDE CHALLENGES AND REWARDS. BELIEVE IN THEM. GET OUT OF THEIR WAY AND THEY'LL KNOCK YOUR SOCKS OFF.

Mary Ann Allison

I AM ENOUGH OF AN ARTIST TO DRAW FREELY UPON MY IMAGINATION. IMAGINATION IS MORE IMPORTANT THAN KNOWLEDGE. KNOWLEDGE IS LIMITED. IMAGINATION ENCIRCLES THE WORLD.

Albert Einstein

1879–1955, German-born American Physicist

IT IS A COMMON EXPERIENCE THAT A PROBLEM
DIFFICULT AT NIGHT IS RESOLVED IN THE MORNING
AFTER THE COMMITTEE OF SLEEP
HAS WORKED ON IT.

John Steinbeck

1902–1968, American Novelist, Writer

WHEN EVERY PHYSICAL AND MENTAL RESOURCE IS
FOCUSED, ONE'S POWER TO SOLVE A
PROBLEM MULTIPLIES TREMENDOUSLY.

Norman Vincent Peale

1898–1993, American Protestant Clergyman, Writer

SOMETIMES IT IS BETTER TO ASK SOME OF
THE QUESTIONS THAN TO KNOW ALL
THE ANSWERS.

Unknown

IF EACH ONE DOES THEIR DUTY AS AN INDIVIDUAL AND IF EACH
ONE WORKS IN THEIR OWN PROPER VOCATION, IT WILL BE
RIGHT WITH THE WHOLE.

Johann Wolfgang von Goethe

1749–1832, German Playwright, Poet, Novelist

WHEN YOU EXPECT TO BE REWARDED FOR YOUR EFFORTS, THEN THE WORK WON'T SEEM OVERWHELMING. WHEN YOU EXPECT TO TRIUMPH, THE OBSTACLES ARE NOT NEARLY SO DIFFICULT TO OVERCOME.

Ralph S. Marston Jr.

NOTHING WILL WORK UNLESS YOU DO.

John Wooden

b. 1910, American Basketball Player, Coach

IT IS NOT ENOUGH TO AIM, YOU MUST HIT.

Unknown

SOME GREAT MEN OWE MOST OF THEIR GREATNESS TO THE ABILITY OF DETECTING IN THOSE THEY DESTINE FOR THEIR TOOLS THE EXACT QUALITY OF STRENGTH THAT MATTERS FOR THEIR WORK.

Joseph Conrad

1857–1924, English Novelist

THE IMPORTANT THING IS TO NEVER STOP QUESTIONING.

Unknown

YOU CAN MAKE MORE FRIENDS IN TWO MONTHS BY BECOMING INTERESTED IN OTHER PEOPLE THAN YOU CAN IN TWO YEARS BY TRYING TO GET OTHER PEOPLE INTERESTED IN YOU.

Dale Carnegie

1888–1955, American Lecturer, Author

TRUST MEN AND THEY WILL BE TRUE TO YOU; TREAT THEM GREATLY AND THEY WILL SHOW THEMSELVES GREAT.

Ralph Waldo Emerson

1803–1882, American Poet, Essayist

DOST THOU LOVE LIFE? THEN DO NOT SQUANDER TIME; FOR THAT'S THE STUFF LIFE IS MADE OF.

Benjamin Franklin

1706–1790, American Scientist, Publisher, Diplomat

IT TAKES LESS TIME TO DO A THING RIGHT, THAN IT DOES TO EXPLAIN WHY YOU DID IT WRONG.

Henry Wadsworth Longfellow

1807–1882, American Poet

PRACTICE GOLDEN RULE 1 OF MANAGEMENT IN EVERYTHING YOU DO. MANAGE OTHERS THE WAY YOU WOULD LIKE TO BE MANAGED.

Brian Tracy

Canadian-born American Author, Business Coach, Motivational Speaker

TRUST

ABRAHAM LINCOLN served as the sixteenth president of the United States during one of the most critical and difficult times for the country—the Civil War (1861–1865). His service as president lasted from 1861 until 15 April 1865 when John Wilkes Booth assassinated him.

Lincoln said so much with so few words. In his brilliant inaugural address, he concisely warned the south: "In your hands, my dissatisfied fellow countrymen, and not in mine, is the momentous issue of civil war. The government will not assail you—you have no oath registered in Heaven to destroy the government, while I shall have the most solemn one to preserve, protect and defend it."

Lincoln started from humble beginnings and worked diligently to learn how to read and write. He worked at many jobs before he ended up in the Illinois legislature where he spent eight years. He also worked as a lawyer and a judge while running for public office.

Lincoln lost several local elections before he was elected president in 1860. As the first Republican president, Lincoln strengthened the Republican Party. In 1863 he issued the Emancipation Proclamation, declaring freedom for slaves within the confederate territory.

Dedicating the military cemetery at Gettysburg on 19 November 1863, Lincoln said, "that we here highly resolve that these dead shall not have died in vain—that this nation, under God, shall have a new birth of freedom—and that government of the people, by the people, for the people, shall not perish from the earth."

In his second inaugural address, now inscribed on the wall of the Lincoln Memorial in Washington, D.C., he said, "with malice toward none, with clarity for all, with firmness in the right, as God gives us to see the right, let us strive on to finish the work we are in; to bind up the nation's wounds."

In everything that Lincoln did, one can see the trust and faith he had in his fellow man.

THE PROBABILITY THAT WE MAY FAIL IN THE STRUGGLE OUGHT NOT TO DETER US FROM THE SUPPORT OF A CAUSE WE BELIEVE TO BE JUST.

Abraham Lincoln

IF YOU DON'T BELIEVE YOURSELF, HOW CAN YOU ASK OTHERS TO DO SO?

Unknown

THE CHIEF LESSON I HAVE LEARNED IN A LONG LIFE IS THAT THE ONLY WAY TO MAKE A MAN TRUSTWORTHY IS TO TRUST HIM; AND THE SUREST WAY TO MAKE HIM UNTRUSTWORTHY IS TO DISTRUST HIM AND SHOW YOUR DISTRUST.

Henry L. Stimson

TRUST IS THE LUBRICATION THAT MAKES IT POSSIBLE FOR ORGANIZATIONS TO WORK.

Warren G. Bennis

American Writer, Lecturer, Professor

TRUST IN THE PERSON'S PROMISE WHO DARES TO REFUSE WHAT THEY FEAR THEY CANNOT PERFORM.

Charles Haddon Spurgeon

TRUST INSTINCT TO THE END, EVEN THOUGH YOU CAN GIVE NO REASON.

Ralph Waldo Emerson

1803–1882, American Poet, Essayist

IN HELPING OTHERS, WE SHALL HELP OURSELVES, FOR WHATEVER GOOD WE GIVE OUT COMPLETES THE CIRCLE AND COMES BACK TO US.

Flora Edwards

I HAVE SELDOM KNOWN A PERSON WHO DESERTED THE TRUTH IN TRIFLES AND THEN COULD BE TRUSTED IN MATTERS OF IMPORTANCE.

Babe Paley

WHEN YOU COME TO THE EDGE OF ALL THE LIGHT YOU KNOW, AND ARE ABOUT TO STEP OFF INTO DARKNESS OF THE UNKNOWN, FAITH IS KNOWING ONE OF TWO THINGS WILL HAPPEN: THERE WILL BE SOMETHING SOLID TO STAND ON, OR YOU WILL BE TAUGHT HOW TO FLY.

Barbara J. Winter

TRUST IN GOD. BELIEVE IN YOURSELF. DARE TO DREAM.

Robert H. Schuller

b. 1926, American Reformed Church Minister, Entrepreneur, Author

TRUST CANNOT THRIVE IN AN ENVIRONMENT WHERE WE PREACH TEAMWORK AND COOPERATION, BUT SELDOM RECOGNIZE OR REWARD IT.

Wayne R. Bills

THE ONE THING THAT DOESN'T ABIDE BY MAJORITY RULE IS A PERSON'S CONSCIENCE.

Harper Lee

b. 1926, American Writer

IT IS BETTER TO SUFFER WRONG THAN TO DO IT, AND HAPPIER TO BE SOMETIMES CHEATED THAN NOT TO TRUST.

Samuel Johnson

1709–1784, English Poet, Critic, Writer, Lexicographer

A PERSON WHO TRUSTS NO ONE CAN'T BE TRUSTED.

Jerome Blattner

TRUST ONE WHO HAS GONE THROUGH IT.

Virgil

70–19 BC, Roman Poet, Author

INFLUENCE IS A MATTER OF TRUST AND ATTRACTION . . . PEOPLE ARE ATTRACTED TO WHO YOU ARE . . . AND TRUST WHERE YOU ARE GOING . . .

Doug Firebaugh

TRUST THYSELF ONLY, AND ANOTHER SHALL NOT BETRAY THEE.

Thomas Fuller

1608–1661, British Clergyman, Writer

ONCE YOU MAKE A DECISION, THE UNIVERSE CONSPIRES TO MAKE IT HAPPEN.

Ralph Waldo Emerson

1803–1882, American Poet, Essayist

DO NOT TRUST ALL MEN, BUT TRUST MEN OF WORTH; THE FORMER COURSE IS SILLY, THE LATTER A MARK OF PRUDENCE.

Democritus

460–370 BC, Greek Philosopher

RATHER FAIL WITH HONOR THAN SUCCEED BY FRAUD.

Sophocles

495–406 BC, Greek Tragic Poet

ONCE YOU GET RID OF THE IDEA THAT YOU MUST PLEASE OTHER PEOPLE BEFORE YOU PLEASE YOURSELF, AND YOU BEGIN TO FOLLOW YOUR OWN INSTINCTS—ONLY THEN CAN YOU BE SUCCESSFUL. YOU BECOME MORE SATISFIED, AND WHEN YOU ARE, OTHER PEOPLE TEND TO BE SATISFIED WITH WHAT YOU DO.

Raquel Welch

b. 1940, American Actress

WHAT IS A FRIEND? A SINGLE SOUL DWELLING IN TWO BODIES.

Aristotle

384–322 BC, Greek Philosopher, Scientist, Physician

YOU MAY BE DECEIVED IF YOU TRUST TOO MUCH, BUT YOU WILL LIVE IN TORMENT IF YOU DO NOT TRUST ENOUGH.

Frank Crane

HE IS A WISE MAN WHO DOES NOT GRIEVE FOR THE THINGS WHICH HE HAS NOT, BUT REJOICES FOR THOSE WHICH HE HAS.

Epicurus

341 270 BC, Greek Philosopher

TRUST, BUT VERIFY.

Russian Proverb

THERE ARE TWO KINDS OF PEOPLE; THOSE YOU CAN COUNT ON AND THOSE YOU CAN'T.

Unknown

A MAN WHO DOESN'T TRUST HIMSELF CAN NEVER TRULY TRUST ANYONE ELSE.

Cardinal de Retz

THE TOUGHEST THING ABOUT THE POWER OF TRUST IS THAT IT'S VERY DIFFICULT TO BUILD AND VERY EASY TO DESTROY. THE ESSENCE OF TRUST BUILDING IS TO EMPHASIZE THE SIMILARITIES BETWEEN YOU AND THE CUSTOMER.

Thomas J. Watson

1874–1956, American Entrepreneur, Founder of IBM

THE MAN WHO TRUSTS MEN WILL MAKE FEWER MISTAKES THAN HE WHO DISTRUSTS THEM.

Camillo Benso Cavour

1810–1861, Piedmontese Statesman, Premier

DON'T TRUST THE PERSON WHO HAS BROKEN FAITH ONCE.

William Shakespeare

1564—1616, British Poet, Essayist

TRUST YOUR OWN INSTINCT. YOUR MISTAKES MIGHT AS WELL BE YOUR OWN, INSTEAD OF SOMEONE ELSE'S.

Billy Wilder

1906—2002, Austrian-born American Film Director, Producer

THE HIGHEST COMPACT WE CAN MAKE WITH OUR FELLOW IS: "LET THERE BE TRUTH BETWEEN US TWO FOREVERMORE."

Ralph Waldo Emerson

1803—1882, American Poet, Essayist

YOU MUST TRUST AND BELIEVE IN PEOPLE OR LIFE BECOMES IMPOSSIBLE.

Anton Chekhov

1860—1904, Russian Playwright, Short Story Writer

FAITH

MOTHER TERESA traveled to Calcutta, India, to teach and to help the destitute and to give them some dignity.

Born in Roman Catholic Albania in 1910, she immigrated to Ireland at the age of eighteen to enter the convent of the Sisters of Loreto. They sent her to Calcutta in 1929 as a teacher. Soon she wanted to leave teaching and start a mission in the slums.

Mother Teresa had to make a choice between teaching and starting a mission for the destitute. Starting the mission with no funds called for complete faith to be able to proceed. She had to depend on prayers and faith to raise money. She was able to get the financial support she needed and also, to her amazement, volunteer helpers including doctors.

This success allowed her work to begin and soon it expanded into Asia, Africa, and Latin America. Later the expansion reached Europe, North America and Australia where the mission cares for the homeless, shut-ins and AIDS victims.

By 1990 there were over one million workers in more than forty countries following Mother Teresa's example by caring for the destitute.

LET NO ONE EVER COME TO YOU WITHOUT LEAVING BETTER AND HAPPIER. BE THE LIVING EXPRESSION OF GOD'S KINDNESS: KINDNESS IN YOUR FACE, KINDNESS IN YOUR EYES, KINDNESS IN YOUR SMILE.

Mother Teresa

BE COURAGEOUS. I HAVE SEEN MANY DEPRESSIONS IN
BUSINESS. ALWAYS AMERICA HAS EMERGED FROM THESE
STRONGER AND MORE PROSPEROUS. BE BRAVE AS YOUR
FATHERS BEFORE YOU. HAVE FAITH! GO FORWARD!

Thomas A. Edison

1847–1931, American Inventor, Entrepreneur, Founder of GE

THE ABLEST MEN IN ALL WALKS OF MODERN LIFE ARE MEN OF
FAITH. MOST OF THEM HAVE MUCH MORE FAITH THAN THEY
THEMSELVES REALIZE.

Bruce Barton

1886–1967, American Congressman

IN ACTUAL LIFE EVERY GREAT ENTERPRISE BEGINS WITH
AND TAKES ITS FIRST FORWARD
STEP IN FAITH.

Friedrich Schlegel

1772–1829, German Writer, Critic

THE BEGINNING OF ANXIETY IS THE END OF FAITH,
AND THE BEGINNING OF TRUE FAITH IS
THE END OF ANXIETY.

George Mueller

ALL THE STRENGTH AND FORCE OF MAN COMES FROM HIS
FAITH IN THINGS UNSEEN. HE WHO BELIEVES IS STRONG; HE
WHO DOUBTS IS WEAK. STRONG CONVICTIONS
PRECEDE GREAT ACTIONS.

James Freeman Clarke

FAITH IS A PASSIONATE
INTUITION.

William Wordsworth

1770–1850, English Poet

THE MORE I STUDY NATURE, THE MORE I AM AMAZED
AT THE CREATOR.

Louis Pasteur

1822–1895, French Chemist

THERE IS NO SUCH THING AS A LACK OF FAITH. WE ALL HAVE
PLENTY OF FAITH, IT'S JUST THAT WE HAVE FAITH IN THE
WRONG THINGS. WE HAVE FAITH IN WHAT CAN'T BE DONE
RATHER THAN WHAT CAN BE DONE. WE HAVE FAITH IN LACK
RATHER THAN ABUNDANCE BUT THERE IS NO LACK OF FAITH.
FAITH IS A LAW.

Eric Butterworth

1916–2003, Canadian-born American Minister, Author

**IT'S FAITH IN SOMETHING AND ENTHUSIASM
FOR SOMETHING THAT MAKES
LIFE WORTH LIVING.**

Oliver Wendell Holmes

1809–1894, American Physician, Poet, Humorist

**FAITH HAS TO DO WITH THINGS THAT ARE NOT SEEN,
AND HOPE WITH THINGS THAT
ARE NOT IN HAND.**

Saint Thomas Aquinas

**IT'S EASY TO HAVE FAITH IN YOURSELF AND HAVE DISCIPLINE
WHEN YOU'RE A WINNER, WHEN YOU'RE NUMBER ONE. WHAT
YOU'VE GOT TO HAVE IS FAITH AND DISCIPLINE WHEN YOU'RE
NOT YET A WINNER.**

Vince Lombardi

1913–1970, American Football Coach

**FAITH IS OFTEN STRENGTHENED RIGHT AT THE PLACE OF
DISAPPOINTMENT.**

Rodney McBride

FAITH IN ONESELF . . . IS THE BEST AND SAFEST COURSE.

Michelangelo

1475–1564, Italian Sculptor, Painter, Architect, Poet

WHEN I DON'T UNDERSTAND SOMETHING, I REACH UP AND HOLD GOD'S HAND. AND WE WALK TOGETHER IN SILENCE.

Ron Atchison

FAITH IS SPIRITUALIZED IMAGINATION.

Henry Ward Beecher

1813–1887, American Congregational Minister, Author

ONE PERSON CAN MAKE A DIFFERENCE. YOU DON'T HAVE TO BE A BIG SHOT. YOU DON'T HAVE TO HAVE A LOT OF INFLUENCE. YOU JUST HAVE TO HAVE FAITH IN YOUR POWER TO CHANGE THINGS.

Norman Vincent Peale

1898–1993, American Protestant Clergyman, Writer

FAITH IS AN EXCITEMENT AND AN ENTHUSIASM,
A STATE OF INTELLECTUAL MAGNIFICENCE WHICH WE
MUST NOT SQUANDER ON OUR WAY
THROUGH LIFE.

George Sand

1804–1876, French Writer

LITTLE PROGRESS CAN BE MADE BY MERELY ATTEMPTING
TO REPRESS WHAT IS EVIL. OUR GREAT HOPE LIES
IN DEVELOPING WHAT IS GOOD.

Calvin Coolidge

1872–1933, Thirtieth President of the U.S.

FAITH IS THE HEROISM OF
THE INTELLECT.

Charles H. Parkhurst

WHAT I AM ACTUALLY SAYING IS THAT WE NEED TO BE
WILLING TO LET OUR INTUITION GUIDE US, AND THEN
BE WILLING TO FOLLOW THAT GUIDANCE
DIRECTLY AND FEARLESSLY.

Shakti Gawain

WHEN I DESPAIR, I REMEMBER THAT ALL THROUGH HISTORY
THE WAYS OF TRUTH AND LOVE HAVE ALWAYS WON. THERE
HAVE BEEN TYRANTS, AND MURDERERS, AND FOR A TIME THEY
CAN SEEM INVINCIBLE, BUT IN THE END THEY ALWAYS FALL.
THINK OF IT . . . ALWAYS.

Mahatma Gandhi

1869–1948, Indian Philosopher

FAITH, AS AN INTELLECTUAL STATE,
IS SELF-RELIANCE.

Oliver Wendell Holmes

1809–1894, American Physician, Poet, Humorist

I MUST CONFESS THAT I AM DRIVEN TO MY KNEES BY OVER-
WHELMING CONVICTION THAT I HAVE NOWHERE ELSE TO GO.
MY WISDOM AND THAT OF ALL ABOUT ME IS INSUFFICIENT TO
MEET THE DEMANDS OF THE DAY.

Abraham Lincoln

1809–1865, Sixteenth President of the U.S.

FAITH IN THE ABILITY OF A LEADER IS OF SLIGHT SERVICE
UNLESS IT BE UNITED WITH FAITH IN HIS JUSTICE.

George W. Goethals

FAITH IS A KIND OF BETTING,
OR SPECULATION.

Samuel Butler

1835–1902, English Novelist, Essayist, Critic

THROUGH WANT OF ENTERPRISE AND FAITH MEN ARE
WHERE THEY ARE, BUYING AND SELLING AND
SPENDING THEIR LIVES
LIKE SERVANTS.

Henry David Thoreau

1817–1862, American Essayist, Poet, Naturalist

I HAVE NOT THE SHADOW OF A DOUBT THAT ANY MAN
OR WOMAN CAN ACHIEVE WHAT I HAVE, IF HE OR SHE
WOULD MAKE THE SAME EFFORT AND CULTIVATE
THE SAME HOPE AND FAITH. WHAT IS FAITH IF
IT IS NOT TRANSLATED INTO ACTION.

Mahatma Gandhi

1869–1948, Indian Philosopher

FACTS THAT MAKE UP THE WORLD NEED THE NON-FACTUAL AS A
VANTAGE POINT FROM WHICH TO BE PERCEIVED.

Ingeborg Bachmann

IT IS BY BELIEVING IN ROSES THAT ONE BRINGS THEM TO BLOOM.

French Proverb

MY INTEREST IS IN THE FUTURE BECAUSE I'M GOING TO SPEND THE REST OF MY LIFE THERE.

Charles F. Kettering

1876–1958, American Engineer, Inventor of electric starter

OUR FAITH IN THE PRESENT DIES OUT LONG BEFORE OUR FAITH IN THE FUTURE.

Ruth Benedict

1887–1948, American Scholar, Writer

WITHOUT RISK, FAITH IS AN IMPOSSIBILITY.

Soren Kierkegaard

1813–1855, Danish Philosopher

I CAN BELIEVE ANYTHING PROVIDED IT IS INCREDIBLE.

Oscar Wilde

1854–1900, Irish Playwright, Novelist, Poet

CHARACTER IS LIKE A TREE AND REPUTATION IS LIKE
A SHADOW. THE SHADOW IS WHAT WE THINK OF IT,
THE TREE IS THE REAL THING.

Abraham Lincoln

1809–1865, Sixteenth President of the U.S.

AS THE ESSENCE OF COURAGE IS TO STAKE ONE'S LIFE ON A
POSSIBILITY, SO THE ESSENCE OF FAITH IS TO BELIEVE THAT
THE POSSIBILITY EXISTS.

William Salter

IT IS ONLY MERCENARIES WHO EXPECT TO BE
PAID BY THE DAY.

Saint Teresa of Avila

I'VE LEARNED ONLY THAT YOU NEVER
SAY NEVER.

Marina von Neumann Whitman

IF YOU THINK YOU CAN WIN, YOU CAN WIN. FAITH IS NECESSARY TO VICTORY.

William Hazlitt

1778–1830, British Writer

THE HISTORY OF THE WORLD IS THE HISTORY OF A FEW MEN WHO HAD FAITH IN THEMSELVES. THAT FAITH CALLS OUT THE DIVINITY WITHIN. YOU CAN DO ANYTHING!

Swami Vivekananda

1863–1902, Indian Spiritual Leader

FAITH IS THE REFUSAL TO PANIC.

David Martyn Lloyd-Jones

THE ONLY FORCE THAT CAN OVERCOME AN IDEA AND A FAITH IS ANOTHER AND BETTER IDEA AND FAITH, POSITIVELY AND FEARLESSLY UPHELD.

Dorothy Thompson

1893–1961, American Writer, Journalist

FAIRNESS

TED WILLIAMS may have been the greatest hitter ever in baseball and he is certainly one of the greatest players of all time.

As a twenty-one-year-old rookie in 1939, Williams drove in 145 runs. In 1941 he batted .406 and no one since has had an average at .400 or higher.

Before the last game of the 1941 season, he was in a mild slump but his average was .3995. That would have qualified as a .400 season in the record books. His manager offered him the chance to sit out a double header and to therefore guarantee a .400 season. Williams didn't want to go into the record book as a .400 hitter who really hit .3995, so he insisted on playing to make it all fair. In the double header he got six hits in nine times at bat and finished the season batting .406.

During his prime, Williams lost five seasons in order to serve as a fighter pilot in World War II and the Korean War. In spite of this lost time he finished his baseball career with a lifetime batting average of .344, exceeded only by three other players, and an on base percentage of .483, the highest ever recorded.

What many people didn't know about Williams was his sensitive side toward children and those in need. His quiet commitment and devotion to children with cancer was demonstrated by his support of the Jimmy Fund for over fifty years. His visits to children's hospitals touched so many, and very few were ever publicized.

A MAN HAS TO HAVE GOALS FOR A DAY, FOR A LIFETIME—THAT WAS MINE, TO HAVE PEOPLE SAY, "THERE GOES TED WILLIAMS, THE GREATEST HITTER WHO EVER LIVED."

Ted Williams

JUDGE OTHERS BY THEIR QUESTIONS RATHER THAN BY THEIR ANSWERS.

Voltaire

1694–1778, French Philosopher, Writer

WE COULD LEARN A LOT FROM CRAYONS: SOME ARE SHARP, SOME ARE PRETTY, SOME ARE DULL, WHILE OTHERS ARE BRIGHT, SOME HAVE WEIRD NAMES, BUT WE HAVE TO LEARN HOW TO LIVE IN THE SAME BOX.

Unknown

WE ARE ALL ALIKE, ON THE INSIDE.

Mark Twain

1835–1910, American Humorist, Writer, Lecturer

SUCCESS HAS NOTHING TO DO WITH WHAT YOU GAIN IN LIFE OR ACCOMPLISH FOR YOURSELF. IT'S WHAT YOU DO FOR OTHERS.

Danny Thomas

1914–1991, American Actor

TOLERATION IS THE GREATEST GIFT OF THE MIND; IT REQUIRES THE SAME EFFORT OF THE BRAIN THAT IT TAKES TO BALANCE ONESELF ON A BICYCLE.

Helen Keller

1880–1968, American Author, Educator

YOU GET MORE THAN YOU GIVE WHEN YOU GIVE MORE THAN YOU GET.

Unknown

THE GREATEST HIGH YOU CAN GET IN LIFE IS BY HELPING SOMEBODY.

Timothy Stackpole

I ALWAYS PREFER TO BELIEVE THE BEST OF EVERYBODY—IT SAVES SO MUCH TROUBLE.

Rudyard Kipling

1865–1936, British Poet, Novelist

HOW FAR YOU GO IN LIFE DEPENDS ON YOU BEING TENDER WITH THE YOUNG, COMPASSIONATE WITH THE AGED, SYMPATHETIC WITH THE STRIVING, AND TOLERANT OF THE WEAK AND THE STRONG. BECAUSE SOMEDAY IN LIFE YOU WILL HAVE BEEN ALL OF THESE.

George Washington Carver

1864–1943, American Horticulturist, Chemist, Educator

EVERYTHING IS FUNNY AS LONG AS IT IS HAPPENING TO SOMEONE ELSE.

Will Rogers

1879–1935, American Entertainer

A HUNDRED YEARS FROM NOW IT WILL NOT MATTER WHAT MY BANK ACCOUNT WAS, THE SORT OF HOUSE I LIVED IN, OR THE KIND OF CAR I DROVE . . . BUT THE WORLD MAY BE DIFFERENT BECAUSE I WAS IMPORTANT TO A CHILD.

Unknown

HEAVEN GOES BY FAVOR; IF IT WENT BY MERIT, YOU WOULD STAY OUT AND YOUR DOG WOULD GO IN.

Mark Twain

1835–1910, American Humorist, Writer, Lecturer

**YOU CANNOT HAVE ALL CHIEFS;
YOU GOTTA HAVE INDIANS TOO.**

American Proverb

**IF YOU WANT HAPPINESS FOR AN HOUR—TAKE A NAP.
IF YOU WANT HAPPINESS FOR A DAY—GO FISHING.
IF YOU WANT HAPPINESS FOR A MONTH—GET MARRIED.
IF YOU WANT HAPPINESS FOR A YEAR—INHERIT A FORTUNE.
IF YOU WANT HAPPINESS FOR A LIFETIME—HELP
SOMEONE ELSE.**

Chinese Proverb

**A GENEROUS MAN WILL PROSPER; HE WHO REFRESHES
OTHERS WILL HIMSELF BE REFRESHED.**

Proverbs 11:25

**NO MAN IS ABOVE THE LAW, AND
NO MAN IS BELOW IT.**

Theodore Roosevelt

1858–1919, Twenty-sixth President of the U.S.

PLANNING

AMELIA EARHART was a famous pilot in the late 1920s and early 1930s. She set many records for both women and men. She held at least eleven important records including the first woman to fly across the Atlantic in 1928, the first person to fly solo between Honolulu and Oakland in 1935, the first person to fly solo from Los Angeles to Mexico City in 1935, and the first woman to fly solo across the Atlantic in 1932. Over the years, Earhart was recognized for her many achievements and was awarded the Distinguished Flying Cross from Congress, the first ever given to a woman.

Although every one of her flights was dangerous and required meticulous planning, her last flight was the most demanding of all.

Earhart had wanted to be the first woman to fly around the world. She teamed with Fred Noonan, her navigator and friend. A trip of 29,000 miles, it required the best of everything—planning, airplane and weather. They started on June 1, 1937, and by June 29 they were only 7,000 miles from completion.

Along the way they had to deal with inaccurate maps, and now they were facing a particularly dangerous flight to Howland Island, 2556 miles away, a tiny spec in the ocean, only a mile and a half long and a half mile wide. They stripped the plane of all non-essential equipment to make room for extra fuel. Precise navigation and weather were key factors and overcast skies made celestial navigation impossible. The plan had no provision for another form of navigation—probably because there was none.

Earhart and Noonan left in good weather on July 2 but the weather soon deteriorated, and the skies became overcast, making celestial navigation impossible. They made their last radio transmission at 8:44 a.m. on July 3 and were never heard from again.

They did the best planning they could with the tools available but it wasn't enough.

Earhart left a letter to her husband in the event the flight would be her last. In the letter she recognized the danger and said that women must try to do things that men have tried. She was forty years old when she disappeared.

PREPARATION, I HAVE OFTEN SAID, IS RIGHTLY TWO-THIRDS OF ANY VENTURE.
Amelia Earhart

THE GREAT THING IN THIS WORLD IS NOT SO MUCH WHERE YOU ARE, BUT IN WHAT DIRECTION YOU ARE MOVING.

Oliver Wendell Holmes

1809–1894, American Physician, Poet, Humorist

ONE THING AT A TIME, ALL THINGS IN SUCCESSION. THAT WHICH GROWS FAST WITHERS AS RAPIDLY; AND THAT WHICH GROWS SLOW ENDURES.

Josiah Gilbert Holland

1819–1881, American Author

FEW PEOPLE HAVE ANY NEXT, THEY LIVE FROM HAND TO MOUTH WITHOUT A PLAN, AND ARE ALWAYS AT THE END OF THEIR LINE.

Ralph Waldo Emerson

1803–1882, American Poet, Essayist

WHEN YOU'RE PREPARED, YOU'RE MORE CONFIDENT. WHEN YOU HAVE A STRATEGY, YOU'RE MORE COMFORTABLE.

Fred Couples

SUCCESS IS A JOURNEY, NOT A DESTINATION.

Ben Sweetland

American Author

WHATEVER FAILURES I HAVE KNOWN, WHATEVER ERRORS I HAVE COMMITTED, WHATEVER FOLLIES I HAVE WITNESSED IN PRIVATE AND PUBLIC LIFE HAVE BEEN THE CONSEQUENCE OF ACTION WITHOUT THOUGHT.

Bernard M. Baruch

1870–1965, American Financier

SOME THINGS CANNOT BE SPOKEN OR DISCOVERED UNTIL WE HAVE BEEN STUCK, INCAPACITATED, OR BLOWN OFF COURSE FOR AWHILE. PLAIN SAILING IS PLEASANT, BUT YOU ARE NOT GOING TO EXPLORE MANY UNKNOWN REALMS THAT WAY.

David Whyte

A GOOD PLAN IS LIKE A ROAD MAP: IT SHOWS THE FINAL DESTINATION AND USUALLY THE BEST WAY TO GET THERE.

H. Stanley Judd

American Author

IF WE CAN'T FIGURE SOMETHING OUT IN THREE WEEKS, WE PROBABLY SHOULDN'T BOTHER.

Steven Gilbert

American Businessman

TRAVELER, THERE IS NO PATH. PATHS ARE MADE BY WALKING.

Unknown

OUR PLANS MISCARRY IF THEY HAVE NO AIM. WHEN A MAN DOES NOT KNOW WHAT HARBOR HE IS MAKING FOR, NO WIND IS THE RIGHT WIND.

Lucius Annaeus Seneca

3 BC–AD 65, Roman Philosopher

IF YOU HAVE ACCOMPLISHED ALL THAT YOU HAVE PLANNED FOR YOURSELF, YOU HAVE NOT PLANNED ENOUGH.

Edward Everett Hale

1822–1909, American Unitarian Clergyman, Writer

YOU CAN'T INVENT EVENTS. THEY JUST HAPPEN. BUT YOU HAVE TO BE PREPARED TO DEAL WITH THEM WHEN THEY ARRIVE.

Martha Washington

1731–1802, American First Lady

BY FAILING TO PLAN, YOU PLAN TO FAIL.

Unknown

IN THE PLANTING SEASON VISITORS COME SINGLY, AND IN HARVEST TIME THEY COME IN CROWDS.

Australian Proverb

TODAY'S PREPARATION DETERMINES TOMORROW'S ACHIEVEMENT.

Unknown

PLANS ARE NOTHING; PLANNING IS EVERYTHING.

Dwight D. Eisenhower

1890–1969, Thirty-fourth President of the U.S.

ONE OF LIFE'S MOST PAINFUL MOMENTS COMES WHEN WE MUST ADMIT THAT WE DIDN'T DO OUR HOMEWORK, THAT WE ARE NOT PREPARED.

Merlin Olsen

b. 1940, American Actor

THE MOST PREPARED ARE THE MOST DEDICATED.

Raymond Berry

b. 1933, American Football Player

KEEP OUT OF RUTS: A RUT IS SOMETHING WHICH, IF TRAVELED TOO MUCH, BECOMES A DITCH.

Arthur Guiterman

FIRST ASK YOURSELF: WHAT IS THE WORST THAT CAN HAPPEN? THEN PREPARE TO ACCEPT IT. THEN PROCEED TO IMPROVE ON THE WORST.

Dale Carnegie

1888–1955, American Lecturer, Author

THE MOST IMPORTANT THING ABOUT GOALS IS TO HAVE ONE.

Geoffrey F. Abert

I HAVE NEVER YET SEEN ANY PLAN WHICH HAS NOT BEEN MENDED BY THE OBSERVATIONS OF THOSE WHO WERE MUCH INFERIOR IN UNDERSTANDING TO THE PERSON WHO TOOK THE LEAD IN THE BUSINESS.

Edmund Burke

1729–1797, British Political Writer, Statesman

IF YOU KNOW NOT WHERE YOU ARE GOING, HOW CAN YOU EXPECT TO GET THERE.

Basil S. Walsh

BEFORE BEGINNING, PLAN CAREFULLY.

Marcus Tullius Cicero

c. 106—43 BC, Great Roman Orator, Politician

I NEVER THINK OF THE FUTURE—IT COMES SOON ENOUGH.

Albert Einstein

1879—1955, German-born American Physicist

YOU CAN NEVER PLAN THE FUTURE BY THE PAST.

Edmund Burke

1729—1797, British Political Writer, Statesman

THE BEST PREPARATION FOR TOMORROW IS DOING YOUR BEST TODAY.

H. Jackson Brown Jr.

American Writer

IT'S BETTER TO LOOK AHEAD AND PREPARE THAN TO LOOK BACK AND REGRET.

Jackie Joyner-Kersee

b. 1962, American Athlete, Olympic Gold Medalist

SPECTACULAR ACHIEVEMENT IS ALWAYS PRECEDED BY SPECTACULAR PREPARATION.

Robert H. Schuller

b. 1926, American Reformed Church Minister, Entrepreneur, Author

THE METHOD OF THE ENTERPRISING IS TO PLAN WITH AUDACITY AND EXECUTE WITH VIGOR.

Christian Nevell Bovee

1820–1904, American Author, Lawyer

A TREND IS A TREND IS A TREND. BUT THE QUESTION IS, WILL IT BEND? WILL IT ALTER ITS COURSE THROUGH SOME UNFORE-SEEN FORCE AND COME TO A PREMATURE END?

Alec Cairncross

Scottish Economist

I'M JUST PREPARING MY IMPROMPTU REMARKS.

Winston Churchill

1874–1965, British Statesman, Prime Minister

DO NOT PLAN FOR VENTURES BEFORE FINISHING WHAT'S AT HAND.

Euripides

480–406 BC, Greek Tragic Poet

REDUCE YOUR PLAN TO WRITING. THE MOMENT YOU COMPLETE THIS, YOU WILL HAVE DEFINITELY GIVEN CONCRETE FORM TO THE INTANGIBLE DESIRE.

Napoleon Hill

1883–1970, American Speaker, Motivational Writer

MANY THINGS DIFFICULT IN DESIGN PROVE EASY IN PERFORMANCE.

Samuel Johnson

1709–1784, English Poet, Critic, Writer, Lexicographer

PLANS ARE ONLY GOOD INTENTIONS UNLESS THEY IMMEDIATELY DEGENERATE INTO HARD WORK.

Peter F. Drucker

b. 1909, American Educator, Writer

MOST PLANS ARE JUST INACCURATE PREDICTIONS.

Ben Bayol

HE WHO EVERY MORNING PLANS THE TRANSACTION OF THE DAY AND FOLLOWS OUT THAT PLAN, CARRIES A THREAD THAT WILL GUIDE HIM THROUGH THE MAZE OF THE MOST BUSY LIFE. BUT WHERE NO PLAN IS LAID, WHERE THE DISPOSAL OF TIME IS SURRENDERED MERELY TO THE CHANCE OF INCIDENCE, CHAOS WILL SOON REIGN.

Victor Hugo

1802–1885, French Poet, Novelist, Dramatist

IT IS A MISTAKE TO LOOK TOO FAR AHEAD. ONLY ONE LINK IN THE CHAIN OF DESTINY CAN BE HANDLED AT A TIME.

Winston Churchill

1874–1965, British Statesman, Prime Minister

CAREER

JULIUS CAESAR, famous for his rule of ancient Rome, was a dictator who greatly expanded the Roman Empire. A military and political genius, he was also very skilled in planning his career.

Caesar was born in Rome in 100 BC into an aristocratic family without exceptional wealth or influence. He claimed, however, that his mother was descended from kings and that his father was descended from the gods, making Caesar exceptional.

A series of four marriages, each conveniently beneficial to Caesar's career, and many military conquests and political alliances brought Caesar to the position of elected consul in 59 BC.

He started a Roman civil war in 49 BC and forced Pompey from his position as sole consul. He pursued Pompey to Egypt where the Egyptians murdered Pompey in 48 BC. Caesar's famous relationship with Cleopatra occurred at that time.

Caesar assumed the title of dictator in 48 BC and by 45 BC he had his empire established. He was well known as an eloquent speaker and used this skill throughout his career to inspire his troops and politicians.

It was on 15 March 44 BC, the famous Ides of March, that Caesar's career planning fell apart when he was assassinated in the senate by a group of senators who had conspired against him.

Julius Caesar was fifty-six when he was murdered, leaving Rome in a period of civil war for thirteen years.

I WOULD RATHER BE FIRST IN A LITTLE IBERIAN VILLAGE THAN SECOND IN ROME.

Julius Caesar

TIME IS THE MOST VALUABLE THING
MAN CAN SPEND.
Laertius Diogenes

SMALL DEEDS DONE ARE BETTER THAN
GREAT DEEDS PLANNED.
Peter Marshall

THE MOST DELIGHTFUL SURPRISE IN LIFE IS
TO SUDDENLY RECOGNIZE
YOUR OWN WORTH.
Maxwell Maltz

1927–2003, American Plastic Surgeon, Motivational Author

THE MEN WHO SUCCEED ARE THE EFFICIENT FEW. THEY ARE
THE FEW WHO HAVE THE AMBITION AND WILLPOWER TO
DEVELOP THEMSELVES.
Herbert N. Casson

American Author

I WAS TAUGHT VERY EARLY THAT I WOULD HAVE TO DEPEND
ENTIRELY UPON MYSELF; THAT MY FUTURE
LAY IN MY OWN HANDS.

Darius Ogden Mills

THIS ONE STEP—CHOOSING A GOAL AND STICKING TO IT—
CHANGES EVERYTHING.

Scott Reed

b. 1938, American Author, Poet

THE VALUE OF YOUR GOAL IS THE PATH YOU TAKE TO REACH IT.
THE ROCKIER THE PATH, THE STRONGER YOU'LL GROW. MOVE
FORWARD. TAKE ACTION. AND MAKE IT HAPPEN.

Unknown

IF YOU DON'T DESIGN YOUR OWN LIFE PLAN, CHANCES ARE
YOU'LL FALL INTO SOMEONE ELSE'S PLAN. AND GUESS WHAT
THEY MAY HAVE PLANNED FOR YOU? NOT MUCH.

Jim Rohn

American Motivational Speaker, Author

ALL YOU NEED IS A PLAN, THE ROAD MAP, AND THE COURAGE TO PRESS ON TO YOUR DESTINATION.

Earl Nightingale

1921–1989, American Motivational Author

NO ONE CAN CHEAT YOU OUT OF ULTIMATE SUCCESS BUT YOURSELF.

Ralph Waldo Emerson

1803–1882, American Poet, Essayist

VERY FEW PEOPLE ARE AMBITIOUS IN THE SENSE OF HAVING A SPECIFIC IMAGE OF WHAT THEY WANT TO ACHIEVE. MOST PEOPLE'S SIGHTS ARE ONLY TOWARD THE NEXT RUN, THE NEXT INCREMENT OF MONEY.

Judith M. Bardwick

American Academic

THE ONLY LIMITATION IN YOUR LIFE IS THE LIMITATION OF YOUR OWN THINKING.

James A. Ray

NOTHING IS TOO HIGH FOR THE DARING OF MORTALS: WE STORM HEAVEN ITSELF IN OUR FOLLY.

Horace

65–8 BC, Roman Philosopher, Writer

WHAT IF YOU COULD BE ANYTHING, OR ANYBODY, YOU CHOOSE TO BE? THINK ABOUT IT. WHAT WOULD YOU CHOOSE TO BE?

Nido Qubein

Business Consultant, Motivational Speaker

MAN IS THE ONLY CREATURE THAT STRIVES TO SURPASS HIM-SELF, AND YEARNS FOR THE IMPOSSIBLE.

Eric Hoffer

1902–1983, American Author, Philosopher

WINNING IS EASY . . . ALL YOU HAVE TO DO IS OUTLAST YOUR OPPONENT.

Doug Firebaugh

AS YOU WALK DOWN THE FAIRWAY OF LIFE YOU MUST SMELL THE ROSES, FOR YOU ONLY GET TO PLAY ONE ROUND.

Ben Hogan

1912–1997, American Golfer

WITHOUT AMBITION ONE STARTS NOTHING. WITHOUT WORK ONE FINISHES NOTHING. THE PRIZE WILL NOT BE SENT TO YOU. YOU HAVE TO WIN IT. THE MAN WHO KNOWS HOW WILL ALWAYS HAVE A JOB. THE MAN WHO ALSO KNOWS WHY WILL ALWAYS BE HIS BOSS. AS TO METHODS THERE MAY BE A MILLION AND THEN SOME, BUT PRINCIPLES ARE FEW. THE MAN WHO GRASPS PRINCIPLES CAN SUCCESSFULLY SELECT HIS OWN METHODS. THE MAN WHO TRIES METHODS, IGNORING PRINCIPLES, IS SURE TO HAVE TROUBLE.

Ralph Waldo Emerson

1803–1882, American Poet, Essayist

RESTLESSNESS IS DISCONTENT, AND DISCONTENT IS THE FIRST NECESSITY OF PROGRESS.

Thomas A. Edison

1847–1931, American Inventor, Entrepreneur, Founder of GE

IF YOU DON'T LIKE WHAT YOU ARE GETTING, CHANGE WHAT YOU ARE DOING.

Unknown

THE GREAT RULE: IF THE LITTLE BIT YOU HAVE IS NOTHING SPECIAL IN ITSELF, AT LEAST FIND A WAY OF SAYING IT THAT IS A LITTLE BIT SPECIAL.

Georg C. Lichtenberg

1742–1799, German Physicist, Satirist

PEOPLE WITH GOALS SUCCEED BECAUSE THEY KNOW WHERE THEY ARE GOING.

Earl Nightingale

1921–1989, American Motivational Author

THE INDISPENSABLE FIRST STEP TO GETTING THINGS YOU WANT OUT OF LIFE IS THIS: DECIDE WHAT YOU WANT.

Ben Stein

b. 1944, American Actor, Writer, Lawyer

WE ARE TOLD THAT TALENT CREATES ITS OWN OPPORTUNITIES. BUT IT SOMETIMES SEEMS THAT INTENSE DESIRE CREATES NOT ONLY ITS OWN OPPORTUNITIES, BUT ITS OWN TALENTS.

Eric Hoffer

1902–1983, American Author, Philosopher

A MAN WITHOUT A PURPOSE IS LIKE A SHIP WITHOUT A RUDDER.

Thomas Carlyle

1795–1881, Scottish Historian, Essayist

KEEP YOUR FEET ON THE GROUND, BUT LET YOUR HEART SOAR AS HIGH AS IT WILL. REFUSE TO BE AVERAGE . . .

A. W. Tozer

1897–1963, American Preacher

THE SOURCE AND CENTER OF ALL MAN'S CREATIVE POWER . . . IS HIS POWER OF MAKING IMAGES, OR THE POWER OF IMAGINATION.

Robert Collier

1885–1950, American Motivational Author

LIFE IS NO DRESS REHEARSAL.

Tom Rea

BIG RESULTS REQUIRE BIG AMBITIONS.
James Champy
American Author, International Management Consultant

SURROUND YOURSELF WITH PEOPLE WHO ARE SMARTER THAN YOU.
Tom Rea

TALENT IS ONLY THE STARTING POINT.
Irving Berlin
1888–1989, Russian Composer

IN THE BOOK OF LIFE, THE ANSWERS AREN'T IN THE BACK.
Charles Schulz
1922–2000, American Cartoonist

YOUR WORK SHOULD BE A CHALLENGE, NOT A CHORE; A BLESSING, NOT A BORE.

Hal Stewins

GREAT AMBITION IS THE PASSION OF A GREAT CHARACTER. THOSE ENDOWED WITH IT MAY PERFORM VERY GOOD OR VERY BAD ACTS. ALL DEPENDS ON THE PRINCIPLES WHICH DIRECT THEM.

Napoleon Bonaparte

1769–1821, French General, Emperor

THE PERSON WHO STARTS OUT SIMPLY WITH THE IDEA OF GETTING RICH WON'T SUCCEED; YOU MUST HAVE A LARGER AMBITION. THERE IS NO MYSTERY IN BUSINESS SUCCESS. IF YOU DO EACH DAY'S TASK SUCCESSFULLY, AND STAY FAITH-FULLY WITHIN THESE NATURAL OPERATIONS OF COMMERCIAL LAWS WHICH I TALK SO MUCH ABOUT, AND KEEP YOUR HEAD CLEAR, YOU WILL COME OUT ALL RIGHT.

John D. Rockefeller

1839–1937, American Industrialist, Philanthropist, Founder of Exxon

USE WHAT TALENTS YOU POSSESS; THE WOODS WOULD BE VERY SILENT IF NO BIRDS SANG THERE EXCEPT THOSE THAT SANG BEST.

Henry Van Dyke

1852–1933, American Protestant Clergyman, Writer

EVERYTHING STARTS WITH YOURSELF—WITH YOU MAKING UP YOUR MIND ABOUT WHAT YOU'RE GOING TO DO WITH YOUR LIFE. I TELL KIDS THAT IT'S A CRUEL WORLD, AND THAT THE WORLD WILL BEND THEM EITHER LEFT OR RIGHT, AND IT'S UP TO THEM TO DECIDE WHICH WAY TO BEND.

Tony Dorsett

b. 1954, American Football Player

WHEN YOU ARE ASPIRING TO THE HIGHEST PLACE, IT IS HONORABLE TO REACH THE SECOND OR EVEN THE THIRD RANK.

Marcus Tullius Cicero

c. 106–43 BC, Great Roman Orator, Politician

SUCCESS

DWIGHT D. EISENHOWER, former president and supreme commander of Allied forces in Europe, had a meteoric rise in rank from colonel in June 1941 to five-star general in December 1944. Eisenhower had earned his way through the ranks by impressing his superiors with his thinking, organizational and people skills. This quick military rise was not unusual during World War II, considering the need for a massive buildup of troops and equipment.

Eisenhower's responsibility as supreme commander of the Allied Expeditionary Force for the planning of Operation Overlord would lead to the D-Day invasion of France on June 6, 1944. Although Eisenhower made many important decisions in his life, none would have the importance of the timing of the D-Day invasion.

An invasion force of five divisions of infantry, two divisions of airborne troops, 6,500 ships and 13,000 aircraft were at the ready to invade Europe through France. Eisenhower had the responsibility to make the decision of when to launch this massive armada.

The weather had been very bad and it threatened the air and sea invasion forces. Eisenhower knew it would be impossible to hold a force this large in a state of readiness without destroying morale and risking detection by the enemy.

On the morning of June 5, 1944, Eisenhower was given a weather report that promised a break on the next day. He met with his staff and made the decision to launch the invasion on June 6, 1944.

Much was at risk and very dependent on better weather. Eisenhower made a difficult decision that achieved success.

THE SUPREME QUALITY FOR LEADERSHIP IS UNQUESTIONABLY INTEGRITY. WITHOUT IT, NO REAL SUCCESS IS POSSIBLE, NO MATTER WHETHER IT IS ON A SECTION GANG, A FOOTBALL FIELD, IN AN ARMY, OR IN AN OFFICE .

Dwight D. Eisenhower

AS LONG AS YOU KEEP A PERSON DOWN, A PART OF YOU HAS
TO BE DOWN THERE TO HOLD THEM DOWN, SO IT MEANS YOU
CANNOT SOAR AS YOU OTHERWISE MIGHT.

Marian Anderson

1902–1993, American Singer

READING FURNISHES THE MIND ONLY WITH MATERIALS OF
KNOWLEDGE; IT IS THINKING THAT MAKES
WHAT WE READ OURS.

John Locke

1632–1704, English Philosopher

HE THAT LEAVES NOTHING TO CHANCE WILL DO FEW
THINGS ILL, BUT HE WILL DO VERY FEW THINGS.

George Savile

1633–1695, English Statesman

I DON'T CARE WHAT YOU DO FOR A LIVING. IF YOU LOVE IT,
YOU ARE A SUCCESS.

George Burns

1896–1996, American Actor, Comedian

IF YOU CAN DREAM IT,
YOU CAN DO IT.

Walt Disney

1901–1966, American Motion Picture Producer

ONE DOES NOT DISCOVER NEW CONTINENTS WITHOUT
CONSENTING TO LOSE SIGHT OF THE SHORE
FOR A VERY LONG TIME.

Andre Gide

1869–1951, French Writer

TO ACQUIRE KNOWLEDGE, ONE MUST STUDY; BUT
TO ACQUIRE WISDOM, ONE
MUST OBSERVE.

Marilyn vos Savant

b. 1946, American Journalist

DESTINY IS NOT A MATTER OF CHANCE. IT IS A MATTER OF
CHOICE. IT IS NOT SOMETHING TO BE WAITED FOR;
BUT, RATHER SOMETHING TO BE ACHIEVED.

William Jennings Bryan

1860–1925, American Politician

TO BE WHAT WE ARE, AND TO BECOME WHAT WE ARE
CAPABLE OF BECOMING, IS THE ONLY
END OF LIFE.

Robert Louis Stevenson

1850–1894, Scottish Essayist, Poet, Author

YOU GAIN STRENGTH, EXPERIENCE, AND CONFIDENCE BY EVERY
EXPERIENCE WHERE YOU REALLY STOP TO LOOK FEAR IN THE
FACE . . . YOU MUST DO THE THING YOU CANNOT DO.

Eleanor Roosevelt

1884–1962, American United Nations Diplomat, Humanitarian, First Lady

YOU WILL FIND AS YOU LOOK BACK UPON YOUR LIFE THAT THE
MOMENTS WHEN YOU HAVE REALLY LIVED, ARE THE MOMENTS
WHEN YOU HAVE DONE THINGS IN A SPIRIT OF LOVE.

Henry Drummond

1854–1907, Irish-born Canadian Poet

BETTER KEEP YOURSELF CLEAN AND BRIGHT; YOU ARE THE
WINDOW THROUGH WHICH YOU MUST SEE THE WORLD.

George Bernard Shaw

1856–1950, Irish Literary Critic, Playwright, Essayist

IDEAS ARE LIKE STARS; YOU WILL NOT SUCCEED IN TOUCHING
THEM WITH YOUR HANDS. BUT LIKE THE SEAFARING MAN ON
THE DESERT OF WATERS, YOU CHOOSE THEM AS YOUR GUIDES,
AND FOLLOWING THEM YOU WILL REACH YOUR DESTINY.

Carl Schurz

THE HAPPINESS OF A MAN IN THIS LIFE DOES NOT CONSIST
IN THE ABSENCE BUT IN THE MASTERY OF HIS PASSIONS.

Alfred Lord Tennyson

1809–1892, English Poet

A MAN, AS A GENERAL RULE, OWES VERY LITTLE TO WHAT
HE WAS BORN WITH—A MAN IS WHAT HE
MAKES OF HIMSELF.

Alexander Graham Bell

1847–1922, Scottish-born American Inventor, Educator

THE BEST THING ABOUT THE FUTURE IS THAT IT COMES ONLY
ONE DAY AT A TIME.

Abraham Lincoln

1809–1865, Sixteenth President of the U.S.

THE MAN WHO SUCCEEDS ABOVE HIS FELLOWS IS THE ONE
WHO EARLY IN LIFE, CLEARLY DISCERNS HIS OBJECT, AND
TOWARDS THAT OBJECT HABITUALLY DIRECTS HIS POWERS.
EVEN GENIUS ITSELF IS BUT FINE OBSERVATION STRENGTHENED
BY FIXITY OF PURPOSE. EVERY MAN WHO OBSERVES VIGILANTLY
AND RESOLVES STEADFASTLY GROWS UNCONSCIOUSLY
INTO GENIUS.

Edward G. Bulwer-Lytton

1803–1873, British Novelist, Poet

KEEP AWAY FROM PEOPLE WHO TRY TO BELITTLE YOUR
AMBITIONS. SMALL PEOPLE ALWAYS DO THAT, BUT THE
REALLY GREAT MAKE YOU FEEL THAT YOU,
TOO, CAN BE GREAT.

Mark Twain

1835–1910, American Humorist, Writer, Lecturer

MEN ARE OFTEN CAPABLE OF GREATER THINGS THAN THEY
PERFORM. THEY ARE SENT INTO THE WORLD WITH BILLS OF
CREDIT, AND SELDOM DRAW TO THEIR FULL EXTENT.

Sir Hugh Walpole

1884–1941, British Dramatist, Novelist, Critic

HE WHO IS CONTENT WITH LITTLE
HAS EVERYTHING.

Unknown

MOST OF THE SUCCESSFUL PEOPLE I'VE KNOWN ARE THE ONES WHO DO MORE LISTENING THAN TALKING.

Bernard M. Baruch

1870–1965, American Financier

WHEN THE WINDOW OF OPPORTUNITY APPEARS, DON'T PULL DOWN THE SHADE.

Tom Peters

b. 1942, American Author, Business Consultant

AVOIDING DANGER IS NO SAFER IN THE LONG RUN THAN OUTRIGHT EXPOSURE. THE FEARFUL ARE CAUGHT AS OFTEN AS THE BOLD.

Helen Keller

1880–1968, American Author, Educator

MEN ARE LIKE WINE—SOME TURN INTO VINEGAR, BUT THE BEST IMPROVE WITH AGE.

Pope John XXIII

1881–1963, Pope of the Roman Catholic Church

ONE MIGHT THINK THAT THE MONEY VALUE OF AN INVENTION
CONSTITUTES ITS REWARD TO THE MAN WHO LOVES HIS WORK.
BUT SPEAKING FOR MYSELF, I CAN HONESTLY SAY THIS IS NOT
SO. . . . I CONTINUE TO FIND MY GREATEST PLEASURE, AND SO
MY REWARD, IN THE WORK THAT PRECEDES WHAT
THE WORLD CALLS SUCCESS.

Thomas A. Edison
1847–1931, American Inventor, Entrepreneur, Founder of GE

NEVER TELL A YOUNG PERSON THAT ANYTHING CANNOT BE
DONE. GOD MAY HAVE BEEN WAITING CENTURIES FOR
SOMEONE IGNORANT ENOUGH OF THE IMPOSSIBLE
TO DO THAT VERY THING.

John Andrew Holmes

YOU WILL FIND THE KEY TO SUCCESS UNDER
THE ALARM CLOCK.

Benjamin Franklin
1706–1790, American Scientist, Publisher, Diplomat

LACK OF MONEY IS NO OBSTACLE.
LACK OF AN IDEA IS AN OBSTACLE.

Ken Hakuta

VISUALIZE THIS THING THAT YOU WANT. SEE IT, FEEL IT, BELIEVE IN IT. MAKE YOUR MENTAL BLUEPRINT, AND BEGIN TO BUILD!

Robert Collier

1885–1950, American Motivational Author

AS LONG AS WE ARE LUCKY WE ATTRIBUTE IT TO OUR SMARTNESS; OUR BAD LUCK WE GIVE THE GODS CREDIT FOR.

Josh Billings

1815–1885, American Humorist, Lecturer

NEVER LET THE WORD "IMPOSSIBLE" STOP YOU FROM PURSUING WHAT YOUR HEART AND SPIRIT URGE YOU TO DO. IMPOSSIBLE THINGS COME TRUE EVERY DAY.

Robert K. Cooper

GREAT SPIRITS HAVE ALWAYS ENCOUNTERED VIOLENT OPPOSITION FROM MEDIOCRE MINDS.

Albert Einstein

1879–1955, German-born American Physicist

**EVERYONE THINKS OF CHANGING THE WORLD, BUT
NO ONE THINKS OF CHANGING HIMSELF.**

Leo Tolstoy

1828–1910, Russian Author

**I HOPE I HAVE CONVINCED YOU—THE ONLY THING THAT
SEPARATES SUCCESSFUL PEOPLE FROM THE ONES WHO
AREN'T IS THE WILLINGNESS TO WORK
VERY, VERY HARD.**

Helen Gurley Brown

b. 1922, American Businesswoman

**NOT DOING MORE THAN AVERAGE IS WHAT KEEPS
THE AVERAGE DOWN.**

William Winans

**NO MATTER WHAT YOU DO, DO IT TO YOUR UTMOST. I ALWAYS
ATTRIBUTE MY SUCCESS TO ALWAYS REQUIRING MYSELF TO DO
MY LEVEL BEST, IF ONLY IN DRIVING
A TACK IN STRAIGHT.**

Russell H. Conwell

1843–1925, American Lawyer, Baptist Minister, Lecturer

THE SPIRIT, THE WILL TO WIN, AND THE WILL TO EXCEL ARE THE THINGS THAT ENDURE. THESE QUALITIES ARE SO MUCH MORE IMPORTANT THAN THE EVENTS THAT OCCUR.

Vince Lombardi

1913–1970, American Football Coach

WHAT IS THE RECIPE FOR SUCCESSFUL ACHIEVEMENT? TO MY MIND THERE ARE JUST FOUR ESSENTIAL INGREDIENTS: CHOOSE A CAREER YOU LOVE, GIVE IT THE BEST THERE IS IN YOU, SEIZE YOUR OPPORTUNITIES, AND BE A MEMBER OF THE TEAM.

Benjamin F. Fairless

DON'T LET WHAT YOU CANNOT DO INTERFERE WITH WHAT YOU CAN DO!

John Wooden

b. 1910, American Basketball Player, Coach

THE ONLY CERTAIN MEANS IS TO RENDER MORE AND BETTER SERVICE THAN IS EXPECTED OF YOU, NO MATTER WHAT YOUR TASK MAY BE.

Og Mandino

1923–1996, American Essayist, Psychologist

YOU CANNOT CREATE EXPERIENCE.
YOU MUST UNDERGO IT.

Albert Camus

1913–1960, French Novelist, Essayist, Playwright

EIGHTY PERCENT OF SUCCESS IS
SHOWING UP.

Woody Allen

b. 1935, American Director, Screenwriter, Actor, Comedian

HE HAS ACHIEVED SUCCESS WHO HAS LIVED WELL,
LAUGHED OFTEN, AND
LOVED MUCH.

Unknown

TO DREAM ANYTHING THAT YOU WANT TO DREAM—
THAT IS THE BEAUTY OF THE HUMAN MIND.
TO DO ANYTHING YOU WANT TO DO—THAT IS THE
STRENGTH OF THE HUMAN WILL.
TO TRUST YOURSELF TO TEST YOUR LIMITS—
THAT IS THE COURAGE TO SUCCEED.

Unknown

PATIENCE, PERSISTENCE AND PERSPIRATION MAKE AN UNBEATABLE COMBINATION FOR SUCCESS.

Napoleon Hill

1883–1970, American Speaker, Motivational Writer

ALWAYS BEAR IN MIND THAT YOUR OWN RESOLUTION TO SUCCEED IS MORE IMPORTANT THAN ANY OTHER ONE THING.

Abraham Lincoln

1809–1865, Sixteenth President of the U.S.

WE ACT AS THOUGH COMFORT AND LUXURY WERE THE CHIEF REQUIREMENTS OF LIFE, WHEN ALL THAT WE NEED TO MAKE US REALLY HAPPY IS SOMETHING TO BE ENTHUSIASTIC ABOUT.

Charles Kingsley

1819–1875, British Clergyman, Teacher, Writer

SUCCESS IS A JOURNEY, NOT A DESTINATION. THE DOING IS USUALLY MORE IMPORTANT THAN THE OUTCOME. NOT EVERYONE CAN BE NUMBER 1.

Arthur Ashe

1943–1993, African-American Tennis Player

A YOUNG PERSON, TO ACHIEVE, MUST FIRST GET OUT OF
HIS MIND ANY NOTION EITHER OF THE EASE OR RAPIDITY
OF SUCCESS. NOTHING EVER JUST HAPPENS
IN THIS WORLD.

Edward William Bok

1863–1930, Dutch-born American Editor

A PERSON IS A SUCCESS IF THEY GET UP IN THE MORNING
AND GETS TO BED AT NIGHT AND IN BETWEEN DOES
WHAT HE WANTS TO DO.

Bob Dylan

b. 1941, American Musician, Singer, Songwriter

SUCCESS IS MORE A FUNCTION OF CONSISTENT COMMON
SENSE THAN IT IS OF GENIUS

An Wang

1920–1989, Chinese-born American Physicist, Founder of Wang Laboratories

SUCCESS IS THE PERSON WHO YEAR AFTER YEAR REACHES
THE HIGHEST LIMITS IN HIS FIELD

Sparky Anderson

b. 1934, American Baseball Manager

SUCCESS IS NO EXCLUSIVE CLUB. IT IS OPEN TO EACH
INDIVIDUAL WHO HAS THE COURAGE TO CHOOSE HIS OWN
GOAL AND GO AFTER IT. IT IS FROM THIS FORWARD MOTION
THAT HUMAN GROWTH SPRINGS, AND OUT OF IT COMES THE
HUMAN ESSENCE KNOWN AS CHARACTER.

Howard Whitman

IF AT FIRST YOU DON'T SUCCEED; YOU ARE RUNNING ABOUT
AVERAGE.

M. H. Alderson

WE DON'T NEED MORE STRENGTH OR MORE ABILITY OR
GREATER OPPORTUNITY. WHAT WE NEED IS TO USE
WHAT WE HAVE.

Basil S. Walsh

FAILURE

WALT DISNEY achieved great success, creating a gigantic empire of over 22 billion dollars in the entertainment industry, but he had to come back from early disappointment and failure.

Disney was born into poverty, both emotional and economical. His father, never successful, offered no love, but plenty of punishment. This led Disney to leave home at the age of sixteen to drive an ambulance for the Red Cross in France during World War I.

On his return, Disney was encouraged by his mother and older brother, Roy, to pursue an early interest in commercial art. He started a small company that eventually fell into bankruptcy.

He then moved to Los Angeles, partnered with Roy who took care of the business, and he began to prosper. Out of this and early failures came Mickey Mouse and the start of an empire.

Disney commented on the creation of Mickey Mouse, saying, "I only hope that we don't lose sight of one thing—a mouse started it all. He popped out of my mind onto a drawing on a train ride from Manhattan to Hollywood at a time when business fortunes of my brother and myself were at their lowest ebb and disaster seemed right around the corner. Born of necessity, the little fellow literally freed us of immediate worry. He spelled production liberation for us."

Walt Disney died at sixty-five, having overcome failure to achieve great success and pass on a legacy of fun and enjoyment for millions.

YOU MAY NOT REALIZE IT WHEN IT HAPPENS, BUT A KICK IN THE TEETH MAY BE THE BEST THING IN THE WORLD FOR YOU.
Walt Disney

CHARACTER CANNOT BE DEVELOPED IN EASE AND QUIET.
ONLY THROUGH EXPERIENCE OF TRIAL AND SUFFERING
CAN THE SOUL BE STRENGTHENED, AMBITION INSPIRED,
AND SUCCESS ACHIEVED.

Helen Keller

1880—1968, American Author, Educator

NO MAN EVER ACHIEVED WORTHWHILE SUCCESS WHO DID
NOT, AT LEAST ONE TIME OR ANOTHER, FIND HIMSELF
WITH AT LEAST ONE FOOT HANGING OVER THE
BRINK OF FAILURE.

Napoleon Hill

1883—1970, American Speaker, Motivational Writer

FAILURE IS SUCCESS IF YOU
LEARN FROM IT.

Malcolm S. Forbes

1917—1990, American Publisher, Entrepreneur

DON'T BE AFRAID TO FAIL. DON'T WASTE ENERGY TRYING
TO COVER UP FAILURE. LEARN FROM YOUR FAILURES AND
GO ON TO THE NEXT CHALLENGE. IT'S OK. IF YOU'RE NOT
FAILING YOU ARE NOT GROWING.

H. Stanley Judd

EXPECTING SOMETHING FOR NOTHING IS THE MOST POPULAR FORM OF HOPE.

Arnold H. Glasgow

FAILURE IS ONLY THE OPPORTUNITY TO MORE INTELLIGENTLY BEGIN AGAIN.

Henry Ford

1863–1947, American Industrialist

SUCCESS ISN'T PERMANENT, AND FAILURE ISN'T FATAL.

Mike Ditka

b. 1939, American Football Player

LIFE IS LIKE RIDING A BICYCLE. YOU DON'T FALL OFF UNLESS YOU STOP PEDALING.

Unknown

COURAGE IS GOING FROM FAILURE TO FAILURE WITHOUT LOSING ENTHUSIASM.

Winston Churchill

1874–1965, British Statesman, Prime Minister

FAILURE IS AN INDISPENSABLE PREREQUISITE OF SUCCESS. IT IS HOW YOU LEARN THE LESSONS YOU NEED.

Brian Tracy

Canadian-born American Author, Business Coach, Motivational Speaker

OPPORTUNITY . . . OFTEN IT COMES IN THE FORM OF MISFORTUNE, OR TEMPORARY DEFEAT.

Napoleon Hill

1883–1970, American Speaker, Motivational Writer

ACT AS IF IT WERE IMPOSSIBLE TO FAIL.

Dorothea Brande

I WOULD HAVE NEVER AMOUNTED TO ANYTHING WERE IT NOT FOR ADVERSITY. I WAS FORCED TO COME UP THE HARD WAY.

J. C. Penney

1875–1971, American Retail Merchant, Philanthropist

OUT OF CLUTTER, FIND SIMPLICITY. FROM DISCORD, FIND HARMONY. IN THE MIDDLE OF DIFFICULTY LIES OPPORTUNITY.

Albert Einstein

1879–1955, German-born American Physicist

THIS THING THAT WE CALL "FAILURE" IS NOT THE FALLING DOWN, BUT THE STAYING DOWN.

Mary Pickford

1893–1979, Canadian-born American Actress

THE BEST WAY TO HAVE A GOOD IDEA IS TO HAVE LOTS OF IDEAS.

Linus Pauling

1901–1994, American Chemist, Nobel Prize Winner

YOUR CHOICE OF PEOPLE TO ASSOCIATE WITH, BOTH PERSONALLY AND BUSINESS-WISE, IS ONE OF THE MOST IMPORTANT CHOICES YOU MAKE. IF YOU ASSOCIATE WITH TURKEYS, YOU WILL NEVER FLY WITH THE EAGLES.

Brian Tracy

Canadian-born American Author, Business Coach, Motivational Speaker

**A MINUTE'S SUCCESS PAYS THE
FAILURE OF YEARS.**

Robert Browning

1812–1889, English Poet

**THE MOST GLORIOUS MOMENTS IN YOUR LIFE ARE NOT THE
SO-CALLED DAYS OF SUCCESS, BUT RATHER THOSE DAYS
WHEN OUT OF DEJECTION AND DESPAIR YOU FEEL RISE IN
YOU A CHALLENGE TO LIFE, AND THE PROMISE
OF FUTURE ACCOMPLISHMENTS.**

Gustave Flaubert

1821–1880, French Novelist

**WHEN ONE DOOR CLOSES ANOTHER DOOR OPENS; BUT
WE SO OFTEN LOOK SO LONG AND SO REGRETFULLY UPON
THE CLOSED DOOR, THAT WE DO NOT SEE THE ONES WHICH
OPEN FOR US.**

Alexander Graham Bell

1847–1922, Scottish-born American Inventor, Educator

**YOU ALWAYS PASS FAILURE ON THE WAY
TO SUCCESS.**

Mickey Rooney

b. 1920, American Actor

FAILURE

YOUR PRESENT CIRCUMSTANCES DON'T DETERMINE WHERE YOU CAN GO; THEY MERELY DETERMINE WHERE YOU START.

Nido Qubein

Business Consultant, Motivational Speaker

LEAD ME NOT INTO TEMPTATION; I CAN FIND THE WAY MYSELF.

Rita Mae Brown

b. 1944, American Writer

IF WE DON'T CHANGE DIRECTION, WE'LL END UP WHERE WE'RE GOING.

Irwin Corey

b. 1914, American Comedian

YOU MAY BE DISAPPOINTED IF YOU FAIL, BUT YOU ARE DOOMED IF YOU DON'T TRY.

Beverly Sills

b. 1929, American Opera Singer

SINCE NOTHING WE INTEND IS EVER FAULTLESS, AND NOTHING
WE ATTEMPT EVER WITHOUT ERROR, AND NOTHING WE
ACHIEVE WITHOUT SOME MEASURE OF FINITUDE AND
FALLIBILITY WE CALL HUMANNESS, WE ARE SAVED
BY FORGIVENESS.

David Augsnurger

WE PAY A HEAVY PRICE FOR OUR FEAR OF FAILURE. IT IS
A POWERFUL OBSTACLE TO GROWTH. IT ASSURES THE
PROGRESSIVE NARROWING OF THE PERSONALITY AND
PREVENTS EXPLORATION AND EXPERIMENTATION.
THERE IS NO LEARNING WITHOUT SOME DIFFICULTY AND
FUMBLING. IF YOU WANT TO KEEP ON LEARNING, YOU MUST
KEEP ON RISKING FAILURE—ALL YOUR LIFE.

John W. Gardner

1912–2002, American Writer, Secretary of Health, Education, and Welfare

MOST GREAT PEOPLE HAVE ATTAINED THEIR GREATEST
SUCCESS JUST ONE STEP BEYOND
THEIR GREATEST FAILURE.

Napoleon Hill

1883–1970, American Speaker, Motivational Writer

DON'T BE DISCOURAGED BY A FAILURE. IT CAN BE A
POSITIVE EXPERIENCE. FAILURE IS, IN A SENSE, THE
HIGHWAY TO SUCCESS, INASMUCH AS EVERY DISCOVERY
OF WHAT IS FALSE LEADS US TO SEEK EARNESTLY AFTER
WHAT IS TRUE, AND EVERY FRESH EXPERIENCE POINTS
OUT SOME FORM OF ERROR WHICH WE SHALL
AFTERWARDS CAREFULLY AVOID.

John Keats

1795–1821, English Poet

INTEGRITY

ELEANOR ROOSEVELT, probably the most famous and effective first lady of the twentieth century, was an activist for causes such as the abolition of child labor and the establishment of minimum wage legislation.

Eleanor teamed with her husband, Franklin, to support his political efforts, especially after he was paralyzed by polio in 1921.

When her husband was elected president of the United States, Eleanor brought with her a wealth of experience on social conditions and sensitivity and compassion for the underprivileged. Her dedication to the job as first lady was unlike anyone before her. Although her political enemies made her a target, her integrity made her unique and respected by people at all levels.

Probably Eleanor's greatest influence was on civil rights and race relations. She confronted her husband and pressured him to sign orders barring discrimination. While traveling in the south, she refused to abide by segregation that required her to sit in the white section of an auditorium, and she publicly resigned from the Daughters of the American Revolution because they barred the famous African-American singer, Marian Anderson, from their auditorium.

Knowing that many institutions did not offer equal opportunity for women, Eleanor held hundreds of press conferences where she permitted only women journalists. This forced news organizations to hire their first female reporters in order to have access to her press conferences.

Eleanor Roosevelt was recognized for her integrity, patience and uncompromising morality.

IF WE WANT A FREE AND PEACEFUL WORLD, IF WE WANT TO MAKE THE DESERTS BLOOM AND MAN GROW TO GREATER DIGNITY AS A HUMAN BEING—WE CAN DO IT.

Eleanor Roosevelt

NO LEGACY IS SO RICH
AS HONESTY.

William Shakespeare

1564–1616, English Dramatist, Playwright, Poet

THERE IS NO RIGHT WAY TO DO A
WRONG THING.

Unknown

IF YOU TELL THE TRUTH YOU DON'T HAVE TO
REMEMBER ANYTHING.

Mark Twain

1835–1910, American Humorist, Writer, Lecturer

HONOR IS LIKE AN ISLAND, RUGGED AND WITHOUT
SHORES; ONCE WE HAVE LEFT IT, WE
CAN NEVER RETURN.

Nicolas Boileau

I HAVE FOUND THAT BEING HONEST IS THE BEST TECHNIQUE I CAN USE. RIGHT UP FRONT, TELL PEOPLE WHAT YOU'RE TRYING TO ACCOMPLISH AND WHAT YOU'RE WILLING TO SACRIFICE TO ACCOMPLISH IT.

Lee Iacocca

b. 1924, American Businessman, Former CEO of Chrysler

I HATE THE GIVING OF THE HAND UNLESS THE WHOLE MAN ACCOMPANIES IT.

Ralph Waldo Emerson

1803–1882, American Poet, Essayist

THE PERSON WHO PAYS AN OUNCE OF PRINCIPLE FOR A POUND OF POPULARITY GETS BADLY CHEATED.

Unknown

ALWAYS DO RIGHT; THIS WILL GRATIFY SOME PEOPLE AND ASTONISH THE REST.

Mark Twain

1835–1910, American Humorist, Writer, Lecturer

THE TRUTH OF THE MATTER IS THAT YOU ALWAYS KNOW THE RIGHT THING TO DO. THE HARD PART IS DOING IT.

H. Norman Schwarzkopf

b. 1934, U.S. Army Officer

MAKE THE MISTAKES OF YESTERDAY THE LESSONS OF TODAY.

Unknown

THERE IS NO TWILIGHT ZONE OF HONESTY IN BUSINESS. A THING IS RIGHT OR IT'S WRONG. IT'S BLACK OR IT'S WHITE.

John F. Dodge

THE VIRTUE OF MAN OUGHT TO BE MEASURED, NOT BY HIS EXTRAORDINARY EXERTIONS, BUT BY HIS EVERYDAY CONDUCT.

Blaise Pascal

1623–1662, French Mathematician, Philosopher, Physicist

HONESTY IS THE CORNERSTONE OF ALL SUCCESS, WITHOUT WHICH CONFIDENCE AND ABILITY TO PERFORM SHALL CEASE TO EXIST.

Mary Kay Ash

1915–2001, American Businesswoman, Founder of Mary Kay Cosmetics

IT IS BETTER TO DESERVE HONORS AND NOT HAVE THEM THAN TO HAVE THEM AND NOT DESERVE THEM.

Mark Twain

1835–1910, American Humorist, Writer, Lecturer

HONESTY IS THE FIRST CHAPTER IN THE BOOK OF WISDOM.

Thomas Jefferson

1762–1826, Third President of the U.S.

DARE TO BE HONEST AND FEAR NO LABOR.

Robert Burns

1759–1796, Scottish Poet

THERE IS NOTHING WRONG WITH THE MEN POSSESSING RICHES. THE WRONG COMES WHEN RICHES POSSESS MEN.

Billy Graham

b. 1918, American Evangelist

NO MAN, FOR ANY CONSIDERABLE PERIOD, CAN WEAR ONE FACE TO HIMSELF, AND ANOTHER TO THE MULTITUDE, WITHOUT FINALLY GETTING BEWILDERED AS TO WHICH MAY BE TRUE.

Nathaniel Hawthorne

1804–1864, American Novelist, Short Story Writer

IT IS REALLY IMPORTANT TO DECIDE WHEN YOU ARE VERY YOUNG JUST EXACTLY WHAT YOU WANT TO BECOME WHEN YOU GROW UP. IT IS MUCH MORE IMPORTANT TO DECIDE ON THE WAY YOU WANT TO LIVE.

Golda Meir

1898–1978, Israeli Founder, Prime Minister

BE TRUE TO YOUR WORK, YOUR WORD, AND YOUR FRIEND.

Henry David Thoreau

1817–1862, American Essayist, Poet, Naturalist

THERE IS ALWAYS ROOM FOR THOSE WHO CAN BE RELIED ON TO DELIVER THE GOODS WHEN THEY SAY THEY WILL.

Napoleon Hill

1883–1970, American Speaker, Motivational Writer

LOSERS MAKE PROMISES THEY OFTEN BREAK. WINNERS MAKE COMMITMENTS THEY ALWAYS KEEP.

Denis Waitley

b. 1933, American Motivational Speaker, Author

INTEGRITY IS NOT A 90 PERCENT THING, NOT A 95 PERCENT THING; EITHER YOU HAVE IT OR YOU DON'T.

Peter Scotese

IF HONESTY DID NOT EXIST, WE OUGHT TO INVENT IT AS THE BEST MEANS OF GETTING RICH.

Gabriel Riqueti Mirabeau

1749–1791, French Revolutionary Politician, Orator

IF YOU BELIEVE IN UNLIMITED QUALITY, AND ACT IN ALL YOUR BUSINESS DEALING WITH TOTAL INTEGRITY, THE REST WILL TAKE CARE OF ITSELF.

Frank Perdue

1920—2005, American Businessman

RATHER FAIL WITH HONOR THAN SUCCEED BY FRAUD.

Sophocles

495—406 BC, Greek Tragic Poet

DO NOT DO WHAT YOU WOULD UNDO IF CAUGHT.

Leah Arendt

PREFER A LOSS TO DISHONEST GAIN; THE ONE BRINGS PAIN AT THE MOMENT, THE OTHER FOR ALL TIME.

Chilo

560 BC, Greek Sage

THERE IS SOMETHING GREATER THAN WEALTH, GRANDER EVEN THAN FAME—MANHOOD, CHARACTER, STAND FOR SUCCESS . . . NOTHING ELSE REALLY DOES.

Orison Swett Marden

1850–1924, American Author, Founder of Success *magazine*

INITIATIVE AND
EXECUTION

ALBERT EINSTEIN, probably the preeminent scientist of the twentieth century, was selected by *Time* magazine as "The Person of the Century."

Einstein was well known as the genius among geniuses whose monumental discoveries had enormous impact on mankind. Few people understood his theory of relativity at first and even many scientists didn't really understand it.

He was the modern intellectual superstar. His thoughts were applied to the practical, such as the development of the atom bomb before the start of World War II.

He came to the United States from Nazi Germany in 1933 as a refugee. It was shortly afterwards that a group of scientists got together to "out-think the enemy." As a result, Einstein wrote a letter to President Roosevelt urging that he approve the creation of an atom bomb. This resulted in the Los Alamos Project where the scientific greats of the time congregated for this serious and world-changing event. This led to the development of a powerful new weapon that ended World War II and undoubtedly saved the lives of countless soldiers by avoiding the invasion of Japan in 1945.

It was his action that was key to giving us a head start over Germany and ending the biggest and most costly war ever fought in terms of loss of human life and property.

Einstein was famous almost his whole life and at his death in 1955, fearing his grave would become a magnet for curiosity seekers, his executors scattered his ashes.

THE WORLD IS A DANGEROUS PLACE TO LIVE; NOT BECAUSE OF THE PEOPLE WHO ARE EVIL, BUT BECAUSE OF THE PEOPLE WHO DON'T DO ANYTHING ABOUT IT.

Albert Einstein

I'D RATHER SEE A SERMON THAN HEAR ONE ANY DAY; I'D RATHER ONE SHOULD WALK WITH ME THAN MERELY TELL THE WAY.

Edgar A. Guest

1881–1959, British-born American Poet

LEADERSHIP IS ACTION, NOT POSITION.

Donald H. McGannon

d.1984, American former president of the National Urban League Board of Trustees

IN ANY MOMENT OF DECISION THE BEST THING YOU CAN DO IS THE RIGHT THING, THE NEXT BEST THING IS THE WRONG THING, AND THE WORST THING YOU CAN DO IS NOTHING.

Theodore Roosevelt

1858–1919, Twenty-sixth President of the U.S.

WE HAVE TOO MANY HIGH SOUNDING WORDS, AND TOO FEW ACTIONS THAT CORRESPOND WITH THEM.

Abigail Adams

1744–1818, American Writer, First Lady

DO IT! MOVE IT! MAKE IT HAPPEN! NO ONE EVER SAT THEIR WAY TO SUCCESS.

Unknown

EACH PROBLEM HAS HIDDEN IN IT AN OPPORTUNITY SO POWERFUL THAT IT LITERALLY DWARFS THE PROBLEM. THE GREATEST SUCCESS STORIES ARE CREATED BY PEOPLE WHO RECOGNIZED A PROBLEM AND TURNED IT INTO AN OPPORTUNITY.

Joseph Sugarman

American Entrepreneur, Speaker

THE MAN WHO MAKES NO MISTAKE DOES NOT USUALLY MAKE ANYTHING.

Edward Phelps

YOU CAN ACCOMPLISH VIRTUALLY ANYTHING IF YOU WANT IT BADLY ENOUGH AND IF YOU ARE WILLING TO WORK LONG ENOUGH AND HARD ENOUGH.

Brian Tracy

Canadian-born American Author, Business Coach, Motivational Speaker

THE SUREST WAY TO GO BROKE IS TO SIT AROUND
WAITING FOR A BREAK.

Unknown

THE SUPERIOR MAN IS MODEST IN HIS SPEECH,
BUT EXCEEDS IN HIS ACTIONS.

Confucius

551–479 BC, Chinese Teacher, Philosopher, Political Theorist

TOMORROW IS THE MOST IMPORTANT THING IN LIFE.
COMES INTO US AT MIDNIGHT VERY CLEAN. IT'S PERFECT
WHEN IT ARRIVES AND IT PUTS ITSELF IN OUR HANDS.
IT HOPES WE'VE LEARNED SOMETHING FROM YESTERDAY.

John Wayne

1907–1979, American Actor

SOLVE IT. SOLVE IT QUICKLY, SOLVE IT RIGHT OR WRONG. IF YOU
SOLVE IT WRONG, IT WILL COME BACK AND SLAP YOU IN THE
FACE, AND THEN YOU CAN SOLVE IT RIGHT. LYING DEAD IN THE
WATER AND DOING NOTHING IS A COMFORTABLE ALTERNATIVE
BECAUSE IT IS WITHOUT RISK, BUT IT IS AN ABSOLUTELY FATAL
WAY TO MANAGE A BUSINESS.

Thomas J. Watson

1874–1956, American Entrepreneur, Founder of IBM

THE REWARD OF A THING WELL DONE, IS TO HAVE IT DONE.

Ralph Waldo Emerson

1803–1882, American Poet, Essayist

ONE OF THE ADVANTAGES OF BEING YOUNG IS THAT YOU DON'T LET COMMON SENSE GET IN THE WAY OF DOING THINGS EVERYONE ELSE KNOWS ARE IMPOSSIBLE.

Unknown

TURNING IT OVER IN YOUR MIND WON'T PLOUGH THE FIELD.

Irish Proverb

LIFE IS SOMETHING LIKE THIS TRUMPET. IF YOU DON'T PUT ANYTHING IN IT YOU DON'T GET ANYTHING OUT. AND THAT'S THE TRUTH.

W. C. Handy

1873–1958, American Blues Musician

**AN OUNCE OF ACTION IS WORTH A
TON OF THEORY.**

Friedrich Engels

1820–1895, German Socialist, Philosopher

**SUCCESS . . . SEEMS TO BE CONNECTED WITH ACTION.
SUCCESSFUL MEN KEEP MOVING. THEY MAKE MISTAKES,
BUT THEY DON'T QUIT.**

Conrad Hilton

1887–1979, American Hotelier

**GOOD INTENTIONS ARE NO SUBSTITUTE FOR ACTION;
FAILURE USUALLY FOLLOWS THE
PATH OF LEAST PERSISTENCE.**

Unknown

**FOOTPRINTS ON THE SANDS OF TIME ARE NEVER
MADE BY SITTING DOWN.**

Unknown

STRONG REASONS MAKE STRONG ACTIONS.
William Shakespeare

1564—1616, English Dramatist, Playwright, Poet

ONE PERSON WITH A BELIEF IS EQUAL TO A FORCE OF NINETY-NINE WITH ONLY INTERESTS.
John Stuart Mill

1806—1873, English Philosopher, Economist

WHAT YOU DO SPEAKS SO LOUDLY THAT I CANNOT HEAR WHAT YOU SAY.
Ralph Waldo Emerson

1803—1882, American Poet, Essayist

WELL DONE IS BETTER THAN WELL SAID.
Benjamin Franklin

1706—1790, American Scientist, Publisher, Diplomat

THE STARTING POINT OF ALL ACHIEVEMENT IS DESIRE.
KEEP THIS IN MIND. WEAK DESIRES BRING WEAK RESULTS,
JUST AS A SMALL FIRE BRINGS A SMALL AMOUNT OF HEAT.

Napoleon Hill

1883–1970, American Speaker, Motivational Writer

WORDS TO LIVE BY ARE JUST WORDS, UNLESS
YOU LIVE BY THEM. YOU HAVE TO WALK THE TALK.

Unknown

MAN WHO STAND ON HILL WITH MOUTH OPEN
WILL WAIT LONG TIME FOR
ROAST DUCK TO DROP IN.

Confucius

551–479 BC, Chinese Teacher, Philosopher, Political Theorist

WE SHOULD BE TAUGHT NOT TO WAIT FOR INSPIRATION TO
START A THING. ACTION ALWAYS GENERATES INSPIRATION.
INSPIRATION SELDOM GENERATES ACTION.

Frank Tibolt

LEAD, FOLLOW, OR GET OUT OF THE WAY
Ted Turner

b. 1938, American Entrepreneur

DOING LEADS MORE SURELY TO TALKING THAN TALKING TO DOING.
Vinet

I THINK THERE IS SOMETHING MORE IMPORTANT THAN BELIEVING: ACTION! THE WORLD IS FULL OF DREAMERS, THERE AREN'T ENOUGH WHO WILL MOVE AHEAD AND BEGIN TO TAKE CONCRETE STEPS TO ACTUALIZE THEIR VISION.
William Clement Stone

b. 1902, American Businessman, Author

IDEAS WON'T KEEP, SOMETHING MUST BE DONE ABOUT THEM.
Alfred North Whitehead

1861–1947, British Mathematician, Philosopher

FOCUSING ON PEOPLE

DIANA, PRINCESS OF WALES, always kept a focus on people and they kept their focus on her. People identified Diana as being more like the average person than anyone in the royalty. She also had a girlish beauty and charm that everyone found comfortable and believable.

Diana had suffered through a failed marriage and periods of despair. Faced with a decision of how to live the rest of her life, she chose to re-emphasize her support of causes such as a worldwide ban of land mines, a cure and treatment for AIDS, and her compassion for children. She always had a deep commitment to people who were in great need of help. She became the Patron Saint of the sick, the homeless, and victims.

Princess Diana's untimely death in 1997 in a car accident in Paris was mourned by the whole world and its remembrance of her will always be connected to the many causes she actively supported.

After her premature death, a memorial fund was established to receive charitable donations from the public. It was in recognition of Diana's life and the many causes she supported. The fund included multiple children-focused organizations, the Leprosy Mission, AIDS organizations, disability-related organizations and many more. This living memorial to Diana, Princess of Wales, only emphasizes her focus on people.

> I UNDERSTAND PEOPLES' SUFFERING AND PEOPLES' PAIN, MORE THAN YOU WILL EVER KNOW. I'D LIKE PEOPLE TO THINK OF ME AS SOMEONE WHO CARES FOR THEM.
>
> **Diana, Princess of Wales**

EVERYONE WANTS TO BE APPRECIATED, SO IF YOU APPRECIATE SOMEONE, DON'T KEEP IT A SECRET.

Mary Kay Ash

1915—2001, American Businesswoman, Founder of Mary Kay Cosmetics

WHEN A FRIEND IS IN TROUBLE, DON'T ANNOY HIM BY ASKING IF THERE IS ANYTHING YOU CAN DO. THINK UP SOMETHING APPROPRIATE AND DO IT.

Edgar Watson Howe

1853—1937, American Editor, Novelist, Essayist

DO NOT SAVE YOUR LOVING SPEECHES FOR YOUR FRIENDS TILL THEY ARE DEAD. DO NOT WRITE THEM ON THEIR TOMBSTONES, SPEAK THEM RATHER NOW INSTEAD.

Anna Cummins

NO ONE IS USELESS IN THIS WORLD WHO LIGHTENS THE BURDENS OF ANOTHER.

Charles Dickens

1812—1870, English Novelist

LET US BE GRATEFUL TO PEOPLE WHO MAKE US HAPPY; THEY ARE THE CHARMING GARDENERS WHO MAKE OUR SOULS BLOSSOM.

Marcel Proust

1871–1922, French Novelist, Author

WITHOUT FRIENDS, NO ONE WOULD WANT TO LIVE, EVEN IF HE HAD ALL OTHER GOODS.

Aristotle

384–322 BC, Greek Philosopher, Scientist, Physician

LOVE IS THE ONLY THING YOU GET MORE OF BY GIVING IT AWAY.

Tom Wilson

b. 1959, American Actor, Writer, Comedian

AFTER THE VERB "TO LOVE". . . "TO HELP" IS THE MOST BEAUTIFUL VERB IN THE WORLD.

Bertha von Suttner

FOR IT IS IN GIVING THAT
WE RECEIVE.

Saint Francis Assisi

THOSE WHO BRING SUNSHINE TO THE LIVES OF
OTHERS CANNOT KEEP IT FROM THEMSELVES.

James Barrie

THERE WAS NEVER A PERSON WHO DID ANYTHING
WORTH DOING THAT DID NOT RECEIVE MORE
THAN HE GAVE.

Henry Ward Beecher

1813–1887, American Congregational Minister, Author

THE SMALLEST GOOD DEED IS GREATER THAN
THE GRANDEST INTENTION.

Unknown

IF YOU CAN LEARN FROM HARD KNOCKS, YOU CAN ALSO LEARN
FROM SOFT TOUCHES.

Carolyn Gilmore

I BELIEVE . . . THAT EVERY HUMAN MIND FEELS PLEASURE IN DOING GOOD TO ANOTHER.

Thomas Jefferson

1762–1826, Third President of the U.S.

TOO OFTEN WE UNDERESTIMATE THE POWER OF A TOUCH, A SMILE, A KIND WORD, A LISTENING EAR, AN HONEST COMPLIMENT, OR THE SMALLEST ACT OF CARING, ALL OF WHICH HAVE THE POTENTIAL TO TURN A LIFE AROUND.

Leo Buscaglia

1924–1998, American Guru, Advocate of the power of love

FLATTER ME, AND I MAY NOT BELIEVE YOU. CRITICIZE ME, AND I MAY NOT LIKE YOU. IGNORE ME, AND I MAY NOT FORGIVE YOU. ENCOURAGE ME, AND I MAY NOT FORGET YOU.

William Arthur Ward

American Scholar, Author, Editor, Pastor, Teacher

EVERYONE HAS A GIFT FOR SOMETHING, EVEN IF IT IS THE GIFT OF BEING A GOOD FRIEND.

Marian Anderson

1902–1993, American Singer

ONCE YOU HAVE LEARNED TO LOVE YOU HAVE LEARNED TO LIVE.

Unknown

IF YOU WANT TO LIFT YOURSELF UP, LIFT UP SOMEONE ELSE.

Booker T. Washington

1856–1915, American Educator, Reformer

WE ARE ALL BORN FOR LOVE. IT IS THE PRINCIPLE OF EXISTENCE, AND ITS ONLY END.

Benjamin Disraeli

1804–1881, British Prime Minister, Novelist

MAKE EACH DAY USEFUL AND CHEERFUL AND PROVE THAT YOU KNOW THE WORTH OF TIME BY EMPLOYING IT WELL. THEN YOUTH WILL BE HAPPY, ELDERS WILL BE WITHOUT REGRET, AND LIFE WILL BE A BEAUTIFUL SUCCESS.

Louisa May Alcott

1832–1888, American Author

WE DO NOT FALL IN LOVE, WE GROW IN LOVE AND LOVE GROWS IN US.

Karl Menninger

1893–1990, American Psychiatrist

NOTHING THAT I CAN DO WILL CHANGE THE STRUCTURE OF THE UNIVERSE. BUT MAYBE, BY RAISING MY VOICE I CAN HELP THE GREATEST OF ALL CAUSES—GOODWILL AMONG MEN AND PEACE ON EARTH.

Albert Einstein

1879–1955, German-born American Physicist

TALK TO PEOPLE ABOUT THEMSELVES, AND THEY'LL LISTEN FOR HOURS.

Benjamin Disraeli

1804–1881, British Prime Minister, Novelist

IN SEEKING HAPPINESS FOR OTHERS YOU FIND IT YOURSELF.

Unknown

IF YOU ARE KIND, PEOPLE MAY ACCUSE YOU OF SELFISH, ULTERIOR MOTIVES. BE KIND ANYWAY.

Mother Teresa

1910–1997, Indian Missionary, Founder of the Order of the Missionaries of Charity

IF THERE BE ANY TRUER MEASURE OF A MAN THAN BY WHAT HE DOES, IT MUST BE BY WHAT HE GIVES.

Robert South

THE MORE YOU SHARE THE MORE YOU HAVE.

Unknown

LIFE WITHOUT LOVE IS LIKE A TREE WITHOUT A BLOSSOM.

Kahlil Gibran

1883–1931, Lebanese-born American Essayist, Novelist, Poet

THE MORE SAND HAS ESCAPED FROM THE HOURGLASS OF OUR LIFE, THE CLEARER WE SHOULD SEE THROUGH IT.

Jean Paul

PEOPLE ARE OFTEN UNREASONABLE, ILLOGICAL, AND SELF-CENTERED. FORGIVE THEM ANYWAY.

Mother Teresa

1910–1997, Indian Missionary, Founder of the Order of the Missionaries of Charity

TIME IS A CREATED THING. TO SAY, "I DON'T HAVE TIME," IS LIKE SAYING, "I DON'T WANT TO."

Lao Tzu

b. 600 BC, Chinese Taoist Philosopher

LET US ENDEAVOR TO LIVE SO THAT WHEN WE COME TO DIE EVEN THE UNDERTAKER WILL BE SORRY.

Mark Twain

1835–1910, American Humorist, Writer, Lecturer

INNOVATION

SAM WALTON was an early leader in discount retailing and is now known for his Wal-Mart superstores and the lowest prices in brand-name, discount retail marketing.

Walton started Wal-Mart in the less-populated towns in Arkansas and surrounding states and was largely unnoticed until he seemed to come out of nowhere with his innovative philosophy of selling brand-name products at the lowest prices. When he was recognized by *Forbes* magazine in 1985 as the wealthiest man in America, he was mostly unknown.

Walton's obsession was to drive costs out of the pricing cycle and work with the lowest possible margins and the highest volumes. His early recognition of the computer as a powerful tool to control inventory and logistics allowed his company to grow while remaining profitable and continuing to offer the most competitive pricing.

In spite of new competition, Walton's success continued based on his proven formula of lowest costs and prices. He inspired his employees and motivated them to be totally goal focused. The employees who participated in the company stock plan benefited greatly from the stock's enormous success.

Eventually the press and many of Walton's competitors attacked him for destroying the small town merchants. The consumer, however, was always his biggest supporter. He said that he was introducing change that was inevitable and good for everyone.

As an innovator in discount retail marketing using the power of the computer, Walton revolutionized retail sales and opened the door for businesses in all industries to improve their operations and become more competitive and successful.

> ## I HAVE ALWAYS BEEN DRIVEN TO BUCK THE SYSTEM, TO INNOVATE, TO TAKE THINGS BEYOND WHERE THEY'VE BEEN.
> **Sam Walton**

INGENUITY, PLUS COURAGE, PLUS WORK, EQUALS MIRACLES.

Bob Richards

b. 1926, American Athlete, Olympic Gold Medalist

THE DISTANCE BETWEEN YOU AND YOUR DREAMS IS OFTEN ONLY AN IDEA-WIDE.

Vic Conant

American Businessman

I DON'T LOOK TO JUMP OVER SEVEN-FOOT BARS. I LOOK AROUND FOR THE ONE-FOOT BARS THAT I CAN STEP OVER.

Warren Buffett

b. 1930, American Investor, Entrepreneur

ARRANGE WHATEVER PIECES COME YOUR WAY.

Virginia Woolf

1882–1941, English Writer

BETTER TO DO SOMETHING IMPERFECTLY THAN TO DO NOTHING FLAWLESSLY.

Robert H. Schuller

b. 1926, American Reformed Church Minister, Entrepreneur, Author

ANYONE WHO HAS NEVER MADE A MISTAKE HAS NEVER TRIED ANYTHING NEW.

Albert Einstein

1879–1955, German-born American Physicist

MOST OF US HOLD THE DREAM OF BECOMING SOMETHING BETTER THAN WE ARE, SOMETHING LARGER, RICHER, IN SOME WAY MORE IMPORTANT TO THE WORLD AND OURSELVES. TOO OFTEN, THE WAY TAKEN IS THE WRONG WAY, WITH TOO MUCH EMPHASIS ON WHAT WE WANT TO HAVE, RATHER THAN WHAT WE WISH TO BECOME.

Louis L'Amour

1908–1988, American Writer

NO GREAT MAN EVER COMPLAINS FOR WANT OF OPPORTUNITY.

Ralph Waldo Emerson

1803–1882, American Poet, Essayist

THE SUCCESSFUL MAN IS ONE WHO HAD THE CHANCE AND TOOK IT.

Roger Babson

1875–1967, American Business Forecaster, Author

THE PESSIMIST SEES DIFFICULTY IN EVERY OPPORTUNITY. THE OPTIMIST SEES OPPORTUNITY IN EVERY DIFFICULTY.

Winston Churchill

1874–1965, British Statesman, Prime Minister

WHEN YOU HIRE PEOPLE WHO ARE SMARTER THAN YOU ARE, YOU PROVE YOU ARE SMARTER THAN THEY ARE.

R. H. Grant

NO TASK IS SO HUMBLE THAT IT DOES NOT OFFER AN OUTLET FOR INDIVIDUALITY.

William Feather

THE SECRET TO CREATIVITY IS KNOWING HOW TO HIDE YOUR SOURCES.

Albert Einstein

1879–1955, German-born American Physicist

WE KEEP MOVING FORWARD, OPENING NEW DOORS, AND DOING NEW THINGS, BECAUSE WE ARE CURIOUS—AND CURIOSITY KEEPS LEADING US DOWN NEW PATHS.

Walt Disney

1901–1966, American Motion Picture Producer

IF A MAN CAN WRITE A BETTER BOOK, PREACH A BETTER SERMON, OR MAKE A BETTER MOUSETRAP THAN HIS NEIGHBOR, THOUGH HE BUILD HIS HOUSE IN THE WOODS, THE WORLD WILL MAKE A BEATEN PATH TO HIS DOOR.

Ralph Waldo Emerson

1803–1882, American Poet, Essayist

WE MUST WALK CONSCIOUSLY ONLY PARTWAY TOWARD OUR GOAL, AND THEN LEAP IN THE DARK TO OUR SUCCESS.

Henry David Thoreau

1817–1862, American Essayist, Poet, Naturalist

GREAT MINDS HAVE PURPOSE, OTHERS HAVE WISHES.

Washington Irving

1783–1859, American Writer

DILIGENCE IS THE MOTHER OF ALL GOOD FORTUNE.

Miguel de Cervantes

1547–1616, Spanish Writer

IF YOU HAVE AN APPLE AND I HAVE AN APPLE AND WE EXCHANGE THESE APPLES THEN YOU AND I WILL STILL EACH HAVE ONE APPLE. BUT IF YOU HAVE AN IDEA AND I HAVE AN IDEA AND WE EXCHANGE THESE IDEAS, THEN EACH OF US WILL HAVE TWO IDEAS.

George Bernard Shaw

1856–1950, Irish Literary Critic, Playwright, Essayist

DREAMS COME TRUE, WITHOUT THAT POSSIBILITY, NATURE WOULD NOT INCITE US TO HAVE THEM.

John Updike

b. 1932, American Writer

GENIUS IS THE ABILITY TO REDUCE THE COMPLICATED TO THE SIMPLE.

C. W. Ceran

EXCELLENCE IS TO DO A COMMON THING IN AN UNCOMMON WAY.

Booker T. Washington

1856–1915, American Educator, Reformer

YOU HAVE TWO CHOICES IN LIFE: YOU CAN DISSOLVE INTO THE MAINSTREAM OR YOU CAN BE DISTINCT. TO BE DISTINCT, YOU MUST BE DIFFERENT. TO BE DIFFERENT, YOU MUST STRIVE TO BE WHAT NO ONE ELSE BUT YOU CAN BE.

Alan Ashley-Pitt

IF YOU CREATE FROM THE HEART, NEARLY EVERYTHING WORKS; IF FROM THE HEAD, ALMOST NOTHING.

Marc Chagall

1887–1985, Belorussian-born French Printmaker, Painter, Designer

SELF-DISCIPLINE

POPE JOHN PAUL II's 26-year papacy was one of the longest in the history of the Catholic Church. Born in Poland in 1920 he survived World War II and became a strong voice against tyranny and communism. Made a cardinal in 1967, he later traveled and spoke all over the world as pope. He defended the Church in the communist countries and remained outspoken about freedom and moral issues.

Pope John Paul II was truly cosmopolitan in his experiences, speaking eight languages fluently, authoring books and traveling all over the world. He met and spoke with an astonishing number of world leaders. In those meetings he was clear about his messages and disciplined and dedicated to peace and freedom.

In 1981 a Turkish national made an assassination attempt on Pope John Paul II, who later forgave the assassin and visited him in prison. Although a strong and athletic person, John Paul's health failed in the last 10 years of his life, making it difficult for him to travel and speak, but he persevered regardless.

Pope John Paul II will be remembered for his love of freedom, his radiance and charisma, and certainly his continuing fight against communism and its violation of the dignity of the individual.

THE FUTURE STARTS TODAY, NOT TOMORROW.
Pope John Paul II

BLESSED ARE THOSE WHO CAN GIVE WITHOUT REMEMBERING AND TAKE WITHOUT FORGETTING.

Elizabeth Bibesco

1897–1945, British Poet, Author

YOU WILL NEVER BE THE PERSON YOU CAN BE IF PRESSURE, TENSION, AND DISCIPLINE ARE TAKEN OUT OF YOUR LIFE.

James G. Bilkey

AS WE EXPRESS OUR GRATITUDE, WE MUST NEVER FORGET THAT THE HIGHEST APPRECIATION IS NOT TO UTTER WORDS, BUT TO LIVE BY THEM.

John F. Kennedy

1917–1963, Thirty-fifth President of the U.S.

EMPTY POCKETS NEVER HELD ANYONE BACK. ONLY EMPTY HEADS AND EMPTY HEARTS CAN DO THAT.

Norman Vincent Peale

1898–1993, American Protestant Clergyman, Writer

TO BE WITHOUT SOME OF THE THINGS YOU WANT IS
AN INDISPENSABLE PART OF HAPPINESS.

Bertrand Russell

1872–1970, English Philosopher

OBSTACLES CANNOT CRUSH ME. EVERY OBSTACLE
YIELDS TO STERN RESOLVE. HE WHO IS FIXED TO A
STAR DOES NOT CHANGE HIS MIND.

Leonardo da Vinci

1452–1519, Italian Painter, Sculptor, Architect

PATIENCE IS NEVER MORE IMPORTANT THAN WHEN
YOU ARE AT THE EDGE OF LOSING IT.

O. A. Battista

BE SURE YOU PUT YOUR FEET IN THE RIGHT PLACE,
THEN STAND FIRM.

Abraham Lincoln

1809–1865, Sixteenth President of the U.S.

I OWE ALL MY SUCCESS IN LIFE TO HAVING BEEN ALWAYS A QUARTER OF AN HOUR BEFOREHAND.

Horatio Nelson

1758–1805, British Naval Commander

DISCIPLINE IS THE REFINING FIRE BY WHICH TALENT BECOMES ABILITY.

Roy L. Smith

ACCEPT THE CHALLENGES, SO THAT YOU MAY FEEL THE EXHILARATION OF VICTORY.

George S. Patton

1885–1945, American General

PERSEVERANCE IS A GREAT ELEMENT OF SUCCESS. IF YOU ONLY KNOCK LONG ENOUGH AND LOUD ENOUGH AT THE GATE, YOU ARE SURE TO WAKE SOMEBODY.

Henry Wadsworth Longfellow

1807–1882, American Poet

THE DISCIPLINE OF TIME MANAGEMENT DEVELOPS JUDGMENT, FORESIGHT, RELIANCE, AND SELF-DISCIPLINE.

Brian Tracy

Canadian-born American Author, Business Coach, Motivational Speaker

SOME MEN HAVE THOUSANDS OF REASONS WHY THEY CANNOT DO WHAT THEY WANT TO, WHEN ALL THEY NEED IS ONE REASON WHY THEY CAN.

Willis Whitney

CONCENTRATION IS THE SECRET OF STRENGTH IN POLITICS, IN WAR, IN TRADE, IN SHORT IN ALL MANAGEMENT OF HUMAN AFFAIRS.

Ralph Waldo Emerson

1803–1882, American Poet, Essayist

THE SIGNIFICANT PROBLEMS WE FACE CANNOT BE SOLVED AT THE SAME LEVEL OF THINKING WE WERE AT WHEN WE CREATED THEM.

Albert Einstein

1879–1955, German-born American Physicist

A PERSON WHO DOUBTS HIMSELF IS LIKE A MAN WHO WOULD ENLIST IN THE RANKS OF HIS ENEMIES AND BEAR ARMS AGAINST HIMSELF. HE MAKES HIS FAILURE CERTAIN BY HIMSELF BEING THE FIRST PERSON TO BE CONVINCED OF IT.

Alexandre Dumas

1802—1870, French Novelist, Playwright

WHAT WE SEE DEPENDS MAINLY ON WHAT WE LOOK FOR.

John Lubbock

1834—1913, English Biologist, Politician

I HAVE HAD DREAMS AND I HAVE HAD NIGHTMARES, BUT I HAVE CONQUERED MY NIGHTMARES BECAUSE OF MY DREAMS.

Jonas Salk

1914—1995, American Microbiologist

HE THAT CAN HAVE PATIENCE CAN HAVE WHAT HE WILL.

Benjamin Franklin

1706—1790, American Scientist, Publisher, Diplomat

PERSONAL EXCELLENCE CAN BE ACHIEVED BY A VISIONARY GOAL, THOROUGH PLANNING, DEDICATED EXECUTION, AND TOTAL FOLLOW-THROUGH.

Gerald R. Ford

b. 1913, Thirty-eighth President of the U.S.

STAY ACTIVELY INVOLVED IN MANIFESTING YOUR DREAMS AND THE WORLD CREATED WILL BE ONE WE ALL WANT TO LIVE IN.

Jewel Kilcher

b. 1974, American Singer

THE MOST SUCCESSFUL MEN IN THE END ARE THOSE WHOSE SUCCESS IS THE RESULT OF STEADY ACCRETION . . . IT IS THE MAN WHO CAREFULLY ADVANCES STEP BY STEP, WITH HIS MIND BECOMING WIDER AND WIDER—AND PROGRESSIVELY BETTER ABLE TO GRASP ANY THEME OR SITUATION—PERSEVERING IN WHAT HE KNOWS TO BE PRACTICAL, AND CONCENTRATING HIS THOUGHT UPON IT, WHO IS BOUND TO SUCCEED IN THE GREATEST DEGREE.

Alexander Graham Bell

1847–1922, Scottish-born American Inventor, Educator

IN BASKETBALL—AS IN LIFE—TRUE JOY COMES FROM BEING
FULLY PRESENT IN EACH AND EVERY MOMENT, NOT JUST WHEN
THINGS ARE GOING YOUR WAY. OF COURSE, IT'S NO ACCIDENT
THAT THINGS ARE MORE LIKELY TO GO YOUR WAY WHEN YOU
STOP WORRYING ABOUT WHETHER YOU'RE GOING TO WIN OR
LOSE AND FOCUS YOUR FULL ATTENTION ON WHAT'S
HAPPENING RIGHT AT THIS MOMENT.

Phil Jackson

b. 1945, American Basketball Player, Coach

A DIFFICULT TIME CAN BE MORE READILY ENDURED IF
WE RETAIN THE CONVICTION THAT OUR EXISTENCE HOLDS
A PURPOSE—A CAUSE TO PURSUE, A PERSON TO LOVE,
A GOAL TO ACHIEVE.

John Maxwell

1512–1583, Scottish Noble

ONE'S DIGNITY MAY BE ASSAULTED, VANDALIZED, AND
CRUELLY MOCKED, BUT IT CANNOT BE TAKEN
AWAY UNLESS IT IS SURRENDERED.

Michael J. Fox

b. 1961, American Actor

HAVE A HEART THAT NEVER HARDENS, A TEMPER THAT NEVER TRIES, AND A TOUCH THAT NEVER HURTS.

Charles Dickens

1812–1870, English Novelist

AN INEXHAUSTIBLE GOOD NATURE IS ONE OF THE MOST PRECIOUS GIFTS OF HEAVEN, SPREADING ITSELF LIKE OIL OVER THE TROUBLE SEAS OF THOUGHT, AND KEEPING THE MIND SMOOTH AND EQUITABLE IN THE ROUGHEST WEATHER.

Washington Irving

1783–1859, American Writer

THE DISCIPLINE OF WRITING SOMETHING DOWN IS THE FIRST STEP TOWARD MAKING IT HAPPEN.

Lee Iaccoca

b. 1924, American Businessman, Former CEO of Chrysler

CONTENTMENT COMES NOT SO MUCH FROM GREAT WEALTH AS FROM FEW WANTS.

Epictetus

AD 55–c. 135, Greek Philosopher

LET US RESOLVE TO BE MASTERS, NOT VICTIMS, OF OUR
HISTORY, CONTROLLING OUR OWN DESTINY WITHOUT
GIVING WAY TO BLIND SUSPICIONS AND EMOTIONS.

John F. Kennedy

1917–1963, Thirty-fifth President of the U.S.

SUCCESS IS NEITHER MAGICAL NOR MYSTERIOUS. SUCCESS
IS THE NATURAL CONSEQUENCE OF CONSISTENTLY
APPLYING THE BASIC FUNDAMENTALS.

Jim Rohn

American Motivational Speaker, Author

TO TEACH IS TO LEARN TWICE.

Joseph Joubert

1754–1824, French Essayist

IF YOU ONCE TURN ON YOUR SIDE AFTER THE HOUR AT WHICH
YOU OUGHT TO RISE, IT IS ALL OVER. BOLT UP AT ONCE.

Sir Walter Scott

1771–1832, British Novelist, Poet

SELF-DISCIPLINE

HE WHO CONTROLS OTHERS MAY BE POWERFUL, BUT HE WHO HAS MASTERED HIMSELF IS MIGHTIER STILL.

Lao Tzu

b. 600 BC, Chinese Taoist Philosopher

WHEN THINGS ARE STEEP, REMEMBER TO STAY LEVEL-HEADED.

Horace

65–8 BC, Roman Philosopher, Writer

DISCIPLINE IS THE SOUL OF AN ARMY. IT MAKES SMALL NUMBERS FORMIDABLE; PROCURES SUCCESS TO THE WEAK, AND ESTEEM TO ALL.

George Washington

1732–1799, First President of the U.S.

COMMUNICATION

RONALD REAGAN was known as the "Great Communicator," and it was his rhetoric and candor that eventually helped bring the Cold War to an end. He never gave up his goal to lead the free world to victory over Soviet communism.

Reagan's belief in God and country convinced him that stopping the spread of communism was the right thing to do. As president he led the rearming of the military and the development of the strategic defense missile system (SDI), forcing the Soviets to compete, which was not financially viable for them. The Soviet economy was already in disarray from previous high costs of military expenditures.

Reagan's public comments and speeches about the "evil empire" and "Berlin Wall" were voiced for eight years. Margaret Thatcher described it by saying that Reagan took words and sent them out to fight for us. He never stopped trying to persuade the world to think about democracy and communism and then to decide which system threatened world peace. His words kept the morale of the free world high and gave strength to many.

Although Reagan's legacy will likely be the victory of democracy over the Soviet system, his candor and skills as a communicator were also effective domestically.

THEY SAY THE WORLD HAS BECOME TOO COMPLEX FOR SIMPLE ANSWERS. THEY ARE WRONG.

Ronald Reagan

IF YOU WISH TO GLIMPSE INSIDE A HUMAN SOUL AND GET TO KNOW A MAN, DON'T BOTHER ANALYZING HIS WAYS OF BEING SILENT, OF TALKING, OF WEEPING, OR SEEING HOW MUCH HE IS MOVED BY NOBLE IDEAS; YOU'LL GET BETTER RESULTS IF YOU JUST WATCH HIM LAUGH. IF HE LAUGHS WELL, HE'S A GOOD MAN.

Fyodor Dostoevsky

1821–1881, Russian Novelist

THE BASIC DIFFERENCE BETWEEN BEING ASSERTIVE AND BEING AGGRESSIVE IS HOW OUR WORDS AND BEHAVIOR AFFECT THE RIGHTS AND WELL BEING OF OTHERS.

Sharon Anthony Bower

ACCEPT COMPLETE RESPONSIBILITY BOTH FOR UNDERSTANDING AND FOR BEING UNDERSTOOD.

Brian Tracy

Canadian–born American Author, Business Coach, Motivational Speaker

FLATTERY IS THE INFANTRY OF NEGOTIATION.

Lord Chandros

WE FIND COMFORT AMONG THOSE WHO AGREE WITH US—GROWTH AMONG THOSE WHO DON'T.

Frank A. Clark

ALL THE GREAT THINGS ARE SIMPLE, AND MANY CAN BE EXPRESSED IN A SINGLE WORD: FREEDOM; JUSTICE; HONOR; DUTY; MERCY; HOPE.

Winston Churchill

1874–1965, British Statesman, Prime Minister

I WISH PEOPLE WHO HAVE TROUBLE COMMUNICATING WOULD JUST SHUT UP.

Tom Lehrer

b. 1928, American Singer, Songwriter, Mathematician

WHEN IDEAS FAIL, WORDS COME IN VERY HANDY.

Johann Wolfgang von Goethe

1749–1832, German Playwright, Poet, Novelist

ONE THING TALK CAN'T ACCOMPLISH IS COMMUNICATION.
THIS IS BECAUSE EVERYBODY'S TALKING TOO MUCH
TO PAY ATTENTION TO WHAT ANYONE IS SAYING.

P. J. O'Rourke

b. 1947, American Journalist, Writer, Humorist

THE GAME OF LIFE IS THE GAME OF BOOMERANGS. OUR
THOUGHTS, DEEDS, AND WORDS RETURN TO US SOONER
OR LATER, WITH ASTOUNDING ACCURACY.

Florence Shinn

TALK IS CHEAP BECAUSE SUPPLY
EXCEEDS DEMAND.

Unknown

IS SLOPPINESS IN SPEECH CAUSED BY IGNORANCE
OR APATHY? I DON'T KNOW AND I DON'T CARE.

William Safire

b. 1929, American Grammarian, Writer

NEVER DO ANYTHING WHEN YOU ARE IN A TEMPER, FOR YOU WILL DO EVERYTHING WRONG.

Baltasar Gracian

1601–1658, Spanish Philosopher, Writer

ANGER IS ONE LETTER SHORT OF DANGER!

Denis Waitley

b. 1933, American Motivational Speaker, Author

NEVER APOLOGIZE FOR SHOWING FEELING. WHEN YOU DO SO, YOU APOLOGIZE FOR THE TRUTH.

Benjamin Disraeli

1804–1881, British Prime Minister, Novelist

TO ASSOCIATE WITH OTHER LIKE-MINDED PEOPLE IN SMALL GROUPS IS FOR THE GREAT MAJORITY OF MEN AND WOMEN A SOURCE OF PROFOUND PSYCHOLOGICAL SATISFACTION.

Aldous Huxley

1894–1963, English Novelist, Critic

BE A GOOD LISTENER; YOUR EARS NEVER GET YOU IN TROUBLE.

Frank Tyger

FEELING GRATITUDE AND NOT EXPRESSING IT IS LIKE WRAPPING A PRESENT AND NOT GIVING IT.

William Arthur Ward

American Scholar, Author, Editor, Pastor, Teacher

ONE OF THE HARDEST THINGS IN THIS WORLD IS TO ADMIT YOU ARE WRONG. AND NOTHING IS MORE HELPFUL IN RESOLVING A SITUATION THAN ITS FRANK ADMISSION.

Benjamin Disraeli

1804–1881, British Prime Minister, Novelist

THERE ARE VERY FEW PEOPLE WHO DON'T BECOME MORE INTERESTING WHEN THEY STOP TALKING.

Mary Lowry

THE OPPOSITE OF TALKING ISN'T LISTENING. THE OPPOSITE OF TALKING IS WAITING.

Fran Lebowitz

b. 1950, American Writer, Humorist

JUST BECAUSE YOUR VOICE REACHES HALFWAY AROUND THE WORLD DOESN'T MEAN YOU ARE WISER THAN WHEN IT REACHED ONLY TO THE END OF THE BAR.

Edward R. Murrow

1908–1965, American Journalist

AFTER ALL IS SAID AND DONE, MORE IS SAID THAN DONE.

Unknown

IF YOU DO NOT TELL THE TRUTH ABOUT YOURSELF, YOU CAN'T TELL IT ABOUT OTHER PEOPLE.

Virginia Woolf

1882–1941, English Writer

IN ORDER THAT ALL MEN MAY BE TAUGHT TO SPEAK TRUTH, IT IS NECESSARY THAT ALL SHOULD LEARN TO HEAR IT.

Samuel Johnson

1709–1784, English Poet, Critic, Writer, Lexicographer

THE GREATEST LESSON IN LIFE IS TO KNOW THAT EVEN FOOLS ARE RIGHT SOMETIMES.

Winston Churchill

1874–1965, British Statesman, Prime Minister

THOSE WHO WISH TO SING ALWAYS FIND A SONG.

Swedish Proverb

WHEN I'VE HEARD ALL I NEED TO MAKE A DECISION, I DON'T TAKE A VOTE. I MAKE A DECISION.

Ronald Reagan

1911–2004, Fortieth President of the U.S.

NEVER FORGET WHAT A MAN SAYS TO YOU WHEN HE IS ANGRY.

Henry Ward Beecher

1813–1887, American Congregational Minister, Author

THE REWARD FOR ALWAYS LISTENING WHEN YOU'D RATHER BE TALKING IS WISDOM.

Unknown

MAKE A HABIT OF DOMINATING THE LISTENING AND LET THE CUSTOMER DOMINATE THE TALKING.

Brian Tracy

Canadian-born American Author, Business Coach, Motivational Speaker

MOST OF US TEND TO SUFFER FROM "AGENDA ANXIETY," THE FEELING THAT WHAT WE WANT TO SAY TO OTHERS IS MORE IMPORTANT THAN WHAT WE THINK THEY MIGHT WANT TO SAY TO US.

Nido Qubein

Business Consultant, Motivational Speaker

EFFORT

Born Josephine Esther Mentzer, ESTÉE LAUDER was
the daughter of Jewish Hungarian immigrants. She was living above her
father's store in Queens, New York, when she started her own business
selling skin creams formulated by her uncle, who was a chemist.

Lauder worked hard and succeeded in placing her products in Saks Fifth
Avenue in New York City. Her obsession with quality was coupled with
her ability to sell, and she protected her niche with personal selling
techniques that captured a customer base she never lost.

In the early years, Lauder concentrated on training people to sell on a
one-on-one personal basis, giving away free samples. She promoted her
products by getting them in the hands of the rich and famous, who
expected the best. She had insightful planning ability and was able to
motivate and train a strong sales force that helped to build the business.

The company Lauder started in 1946, named Estée Lauder, grew to sales of 4 billion dollars by 2004 and operates in 118 countries, controlling 45 percent of the cosmetics business. She became the richest self-made woman in the world.

Even with all her wealth, Lauder stopped working only when failing health in her later years forced her to slow down. She was still attending new product launches into her nineties. It was this hard work and tenacious effort, along with quality products and selling ability that made Estée Lauder such a success.

I DIDN'T GET WHERE I AM BY THINKING ABOUT IT OR DREAMING IT. I GOT THERE BY DOING IT.

Estée Lauder

NO MATTER HOW DARK THINGS SEEM TO BE OR ACTUALLY ARE, RAISE YOUR SIGHTS AND SEE THE POSSIBILITIES— ALWAYS SEE THEM, FOR THEY'RE ALWAYS THERE.

Norman Vincent Peale

1898–1993, American Protestant Clergyman, Writer

THE ONLY MAN WHO MAKES NO MISTAKES IS THE MAN WHO NEVER DOES ANYTHING.

Eleanor Roosevelt

1884–1962, American United Nations Diplomat, Humanitarian, First Lady

AN ETHICAL PERSON OUGHT TO DO MORE THAN HE'S REQUIRED TO DO AND LESS THAN HE'S ALLOWED TO DO.

Michael Josephson

NOTHING WILL WORK UNLESS YOU DO.

John Wooden

b. 1910, American Basketball Player, Coach

THE HIGHEST REWARD FOR A PERSON'S TOIL IS NOT WHAT THEY GET FOR IT, BUT WHAT THEY BECOME BY IT.

John Ruskin

1819–1900, English Writer, Art Critic, Architecture Critic

I DO THE BEST I KNOW HOW, THE VERY BEST I CAN: AND I MEAN TO KEEP ON DOING IT TO THE END. IF THE END BRINGS ME OUT ALL RIGHT, WHAT IS SAID ABOUT ME WILL NOT AMOUNT TO ANYTHING. IF THE END BRINGS ME OUT ALL WRONG, THEN ANGELS SWEARING I WAS RIGHT WOULD MAKE NO DIFFERENCE.

Abraham Lincoln

1809–1865, Sixteenth President of the U.S.

HE WHO BELIEVES IS STRONG; HE WHO DOUBTS IS WEAK. STRONG CONVICTIONS PRECEDE GREAT ACTIONS.

T. F. Clarke

"I CAN'T DO IT" NEVER ACCOMPLISHED ANYTHING; "I WILL TRY" HAS ACCOMPLISHED WONDERS.

George P. Burnham

I FIND THE GREAT THING IN THIS WORLD IS NOT SO MUCH
WHERE WE STAND, AS IN WHAT DIRECTION WE ARE MOVING;
TO REACH THE PORT OF HEAVEN, WE MUST SAIL SOMETIMES
WITH THE WIND AND SOMETIMES AGAINST IT BUT WE MUST
SAIL, AND NOT DRIFT, NOR LIE AT ANCHOR.

Oliver Wendell Holmes

1809–1894, American Physician, Poet, Humorist

I HAVE LEARNED THAT SUCCESS IS TO BE MEASURED NOT SO
MUCH BY THE POSITION THAT ONE HAS REACHED IN LIFE AS BY
THE OBSTACLES WHICH ONE HAS OVERCOME WHILE TRYING TO
SUCCEED.

Booker T. Washington

1856–1915, American Educator, Reformer

WORK SPARES US FROM THREE GREAT EVILS: BOREDOM,
VICE AND NEED.

Voltaire

1694–1778, French Philosopher, Writer

THE MOST PRACTICAL, BEAUTIFUL, WORKABLE PHILOSOPHY IN
THE WORLD WON'T WORK—IF YOU WON'T.

Zig Ziglar

b. 1926, American Motivational Speaker, Author

IT IS ONLY THROUGH LABOR AND PAINFUL EFFORT, BY GRIM ENERGY AND RESOLUTE COURAGE, THAT WE MOVE ON TO BETTER THINGS.

Theodore Roosevelt

1858–1919, Twenty-sixth President of the U.S.

THINGS MAY COME TO THOSE WHO WAIT, BUT ONLY THE THINGS LEFT BY THOSE WHO HUSTLE.

Abraham Lincoln

1809–1865, Sixteenth President of the U.S.

WHAT WE THINK OR WHAT WE BELIEVE IS, IN THE END, OF LITTLE CONSEQUENCE. THE ONLY THING OF CONSEQUENCE IS WHAT WE DO.

John Ruskin

1819–1900, English Writer, Art Critic, Architecture Critic

I HAVE DISCOVERED IN LIFE THAT THERE ARE WAYS OF GETTING ALMOST ANYWHERE YOU WANT TO GO, IF YOU REALLY WANT TO GO.

Langston Hughes

1902–1967, American Writer, Editor, Lecturer

DON'T LET WHAT YOU CANNOT DO INTERFERE WITH WHAT YOU CAN DO.

John Wooden

b. 1910, American Basketball Player, Coach

IF YOU ONLY CARE ENOUGH FOR A RESULT, YOU WILL ALMOST CERTAINLY ATTAIN IT.

William James

1842–1910, American Philosopher, Psychologist

EVEN IF YOU ARE ON THE RIGHT TRACK, YOU'LL GET RUN OVER IF YOU JUST SIT THERE.

Will Rogers

1879–1935, American Entertainer

SUCCESS IS NOT THE KEY TO HAPPINESS. HAPPINESS IS THE KEY TO SUCCESS. IF YOU LOVE WHAT YOU ARE DOING, YOU WILL BE SUCCESSFUL.

Albert Schweitzer

1875–1965, German Theologian, Musician, Philosopher

IF THERE'S A WAY TO DO IT BETTER . . . FIND IT.

Thomas A. Edison

1847–1931, American Inventor, Entrepreneur, Founder of GE

IF IT IS TO BE, IT IS UP TO ME.

William H. Johnson

DO NOT WAIT; THE TIME WILL NEVER BE "JUST RIGHT." START WHERE YOU STAND, WORK WITH WHATEVER TOOLS YOU HAVE AT YOUR COMMAND, AND THE BETTER TOOLS WILL BE FOUND AS YOU GO ALONG.

Napoleon Hill

1883–1970, American Speaker, Motivational Writer

ALL WHO HAVE ACCOMPLISHED GREAT THINGS HAVE HAD A GREAT AIM, HAVE FIXED THEIR GAZE ON A GOAL WHICH IS HIGH, ONE WHICH SOMETIMES SEEMS IMPOSSIBLE.

Orison Swett Marden

1850–1924, American Writer, Founder of Success *magazine*

WHENEVER YOU ARE ASKED IF YOU CAN DO A JOB, TELL 'EM, "CERTAINLY I CAN!" THEN GET BUSY AND FIND OUT HOW TO DO IT.

Theodore Roosevelt

1858–1919, Twenty-sixth President of the U.S.

CHAMPIONS KEEP PLAYING UNTIL THEY GET IT RIGHT.

Billie Jean King

b. 1943, American Tennis Player

ALWAYS LOOK AT WHAT YOU HAVE LEFT. NEVER LOOK AT WHAT YOU HAVE LOST.

Robert H. Schuller

b. 1926, American Reformed Church Minister, Entrepreneur, Author

IT IS HARD TO FAIL, BUT IT IS WORSE NEVER TO HAVE TRIED TO SUCCEED. IN THIS LIFE WE GET NOTHING SAVE BY EFFORT.

Theodore Roosevelt

1858–1919, Twenty-sixth President of the U.S.

I'M A GREAT BELIEVER IN LUCK AND I FIND THE HARDER I WORK, THE MORE I HAVE OF IT.

Thomas Jefferson

1762–1826, Third President of the U.S.

OPPORTUNITIES MULTIPLY AS THEY ARE SEIZED.

Sun Tzu

c. 500 BC, Chinese General

AND IN THE END, IT'S NOT THE YEARS IN YOUR LIFE THAT COUNT. IT'S THE LIFE IN YOUR YEARS.

Abraham Lincoln

1809–1865, Sixteenth President of the U.S.

STRIVING FOR PERFECTION IS THE GREATEST STOPPER THERE IS . . . IT'S YOUR EXCUSE TO YOURSELF FOR NOT DOING ANYTHING. INSTEAD, STRIVE FOR EXCELLENCE, DO YOUR BEST.

Sir Laurence Olivier

1907–1989, English Actor, Producer, Film Director

THE REWARD FOR A THING WELL DONE IS TO HAVE DONE IT.

Ralph Waldo Emerson

1803–1882, American Poet, Essayist

I CAN'T IMAGINE A PERSON BECOMING A SUCCESS WHO DOESN'T GIVE THIS GAME OF LIFE EVERYTHING HE'S GOT.

Walter Cronkite

b. 1916, American Journalist

THE CREDIT BELONGS TO THE MAN WHO IS ACTUALLY IN THE ARENA; WHOSE FACE IS MARRED BY DUST AND SWEAT AND BLOOD; WHO STRIVES VALIANTLY; WHO ERRS AND COMES SHORT AGAIN AND AGAIN; WHO KNOWS THE GREAT ENTHUSI-ASMS, THE GREAT DEVOTIONS, AND SPENDS HIMSELF IN A WORTHY CAUSE; WHO AT THE BEST KNOWS IN THE END THE TRIUMPH OF HIGH ACHIEVEMENT; AND WHO AT THE WORST, IF HE FAILS, AT LEAST FAILS WHILE DARING GREATLY.

Theodore Roosevelt

1858–1919, Twenty-sixth President of the U.S.

GOOD, BETTER, BEST; NEVER LET IT REST UNTIL YOUR GOOD IS BETTER AND YOUR BETTER IS BEST.

Unknown

MOST PEOPLE NEVER RUN FAR ENOUGH ON THEIR FIRST WIND TO FIND OUT THEY'VE GOT A SECOND. GIVE YOUR DREAMS ALL YOU'VE GOT AND YOU'LL BE AMAZED AT THE ENERGY THAT COMES OUT OF YOU.

William James

1842–1910, American Philosopher, Psychologist

NOBODY'S A NATURAL. YOU WORK HARD TO GET GOOD AND THEN WORK HARD TO GET BETTER.

Paul Coffey

b. 1961, Canadian Hockey Player

SUCCESS IS ALMOST TOTALLY DEPENDENT UPON DRIVE AND PERSISTENCE. THE EXTRA ENERGY REQUIRED TO MAKE ANOTHER EFFORT OR TRY ANOTHER APPROACH IS THE SECRET OF WINNING.

Denis Waitley

b. 1933, American Motivational Speaker, Author

CHANGE

OPRAH WINFREY is known for her rapid rise out of poverty and abuse to her status today as a highly successful, nationally syndicated talk-show host. She was only thirty-two in 1986 when she achieved this success.

Before her show was syndicated, Winfrey competed with Phil Donahue, pioneer of the talk-show format, in the same time slot in Chicago. Her unique style moved her into first place in the ratings.

It was her personal touch and new approach to talk-show television that contributed to her success and caused a dramatic change to the talk-show format. Winfrey's conversational style helped her connect with her audience, influencing them with every word that she spoke. Her guests are not only celebrities and experts but regular people who share their own personal stories. Winfrey herself doesn't seem to hold back on personal issues, sharing her joy and sorrow with her audience. It is clear that her fans and massive audiences want to hear what she says and believes.

It's acknowledged that Winfrey's on-air book club has made instant bestsellers. She has 14 million viewers, in the U.S. and 132 other countries, who regularly watch her show.

Now, at age 51, Winfrey has become not only incredibly wealthy, but she is an influential owner of several companies in the entertainment business. She has also succeeded as an actress, winning an Academy Award nomination for the movie *The Color Purple*.

Winfrey uses her influence for good. She has been involved in many charities and almost daily brings happiness to the many people she features on her show. She also encourages her viewers to improve themselves and the world around them.

FOLLOW YOUR INSTINCTS, THAT'S WHERE TRUE WISDOM MANIFESTS ITSELF.

Oprah Winfrey

FLEXIBILITY IN A TIME OF GREAT CHANGE IS A VITAL QUALITY OF LEADERSHIP.

Brian Tracy

Canadian-born American Author, Business Coach, Motivational Speaker

PEOPLE SELDOM IMPROVE WHEN THEY HAVE NO OTHER MODEL BUT THEMSELVES TO COPY.

Oliver Goldsmith

1730–1774, Irish-born British Essayist, Poet, Novelist, Dramatist

WE MUST ALWAYS CHANGE, RENEW REJUVENATE OURSELVES; OTHERWISE WE HARDEN.

Johann Wolfgang von Goethe

1749–1832, German Playwright, Poet, Novelist

WHEN YOU FALL IN A RIVER, YOU'RE NO LONGER A FISHERMAN; YOU'RE A SWIMMER.

Gene Hill

THE THING THAT LIES AT THE FOUNDATION OF POSITIVE CHANGE, THE WAY I SEE IT, IS SERVICE TO A FELLOW HUMAN BEING.

Lech Walesa

b. 1943, Polish Activist, Electrician, President of Poland

AND THE DAY CAME WHEN THE RISK IT TOOK TO REMAIN TIGHT IN A BUD WAS MORE PAINFUL THAN THE RISK IT TOOK TO BLOSSOM.

Anais Nin

1903–1977, French-born American Author

HE THAT NEVER CHANGES HIS OPINIONS, NEVER CORRECTS HIS MISTAKES, WILL NEVER BE WISER ON THE MORROW THAN HE IS TODAY.

Tryon Edwards

1809–1894, American Theologian, Editor

TO CHANGE A HABIT, MAKE A CONSCIOUS DECISION, THEN "ACT OUT" THE NEW BEHAVIOR.

Maxwell Maltz

1927–2003, American Plastic Surgeon, Motivational Author

GOOD HABITS ARE AS ADDICTIVE AS BAD HABITS, AND A LOT MORE REWARDING.

Harvey Mackay

American Author, Entrepreneur, Business Speaker

THE SPEED OF THE LEADER DETERMINES THE RATE OF THE PACK.

Unknown

CHANGE BRINGS OPPORTUNITY.

Nido Qubein

Business Consultant, Motivational Speaker

NEW OPINIONS ARE ALWAYS SUSPECTED, AND USUALLY OPPOSED, WITHOUT ANY OTHER REASON BUT BECAUSE THEY ARE NOT ALREADY COMMON.

John Locke

1632–1704, English Philosopher

FOR EVERY FAILURE, THERE'S AN ALTERNATIVE COURSE OF ACTION. YOU JUST HAVE TO FIND IT. WHEN YOU COME TO A ROADBLOCK, TAKE A DETOUR.

Mary Kay Ash

1915–2001, American Businesswoman, Founder of Mary Kay Cosmetics

WE MUST HAVE COURAGE TO BET ON OUR IDEAS, TO TAKE THE CALCULATED RISK, AND TO ACT.

Maxwell Maltz

1927–2003, American Plastic Surgeon, Motivational Author

IT IS NOT THE STRONGEST OF THE SPECIES THAT SURVIVE, NOR THE MOST INTELLIGENT, BUT THE ONE MOST RESPONSIVE TO CHANGE.

Charles Darwin

1809–1882, English Naturalist, Author

PERMIT NO ONE TO DISSUADE YOU FROM PURSUING THE GOALS YOU SET FOR YOURSELVES. DO NOT FEAR TO PIONEER. TO VENTURE DOWN NEW PATHS OF ENDEAVOR.

Ralph J. Bunche

1904–1971, American Statesman

I AM ALWAYS DOING THINGS I CAN'T DO; THAT'S HOW I GET TO DO THEM.

Pablo Picasso

1881–1973, Spanish Artist, Painter

LIFE IS A SUCCESSION OF LESSONS WHICH MUST BE LIVED TO BE UNDERSTOOD.

Ralph Waldo Emerson

1803–1882, American Poet, Essayist

IF YOU HAVE NOTHING ELSE TO DO, LOOK AT YOURSELF AND SEE IF THERE ISN'T SOMETHING CLOSE AT HAND YOU CAN IMPROVE. IT MAY MAKE YOU WEALTHY, ALTHOUGH IT IS MORE LIKELY IT WILL MAKE YOU HAPPY.

George M. Adams

INDEX